MW01444751

Transitioning Beyond Your Conditioned Blueprint

Transitioning Beyond Your Conditioned Blueprint

A Pathway to Freedom through Self-awareness

Susan V. Kippen

Transitioning Beyond Your Conditioned Blueprint

A Pathway to Freedom through Self-awareness

Copyright © 2022 Susan V. Kippen

All rights reserved. No part of this book may be reproduced or transmitted in any form or by any means, electronic or mechanical, including photo copying or by any information storage or retrieval system, without permission in writing from the author.

Conscious Quest Press – PO Box 165 Manomet, MA 02345

Book cover design created by Leanne Brown

Cover image – Istock.com

ISBN 978-0-9984963-1-3 (paperback edition)

ISBN 978-0-9984963-2-0 (eBook edition)

ISBN 978-0-9984963-3-7 (hardback edition)

Library of Congress Control Number: 2022904423, Plymouth, MA

Disclaimer

This book was created for your personal use as a tool for achieving greater self-awareness. The material contained within is for informational purposes and offers an understanding of a consciously chosen approach for honest participation with the self and all of life.

Before beginning any new program or making use of any information from this book, it is recommended that you seek medical/psychological advice from your personal physician or licensed mental health provider. This book is not intended to diagnose, be a substitute for any support program, psychiatric care, medical advice, or medical care that you are presently receiving or may need from a licensed mental health professional or a licensed physician. Readers should consult with their health care provider in any matters relating to any area of health. The author does not assume and hereby disclaims any liability to any party for any loss, damage, or disruption caused by applied use of information contained in this book, errors, or omissions, whether such errors or omissions result from accident, negligence, or any other cause. If you wish to make use of the information contained in this book, you are taking full responsibility for your own choices.

Most of the examples in this book are a compilation of similar experiences from the lives of individuals. The names in most the examples are fictitious.

The information in this book shall not be reproduced in any form or used for financial gain without the explicit consent of the author.

Acknowledgments

First, I would like to express gratitude for all the insight and wisdom that has come about from my encounters with many people over the years from all walks of life. Without those encounters, many contemplations and realizations would not have been possible.

I also give thanks for the individuals whose encouragement and support on a personal and professional level have led to the creation of this book.

For copyediting, I am grateful to Pam Summa

Also, I am deeply grateful for the wisdom and knowing which has come from my own participation in presence – the Divine within All.

Contents

Introduction..1

Chapter One: Refocusing your Lens

    1. Building a bridge from basic ideas to discovery, in-depth understanding, and a new process...11

    2. How do set ideas, labels, and fantasy-based ideas create struggle, limitation, and suffering?..................................13

        Steps for transitioning from a basic idea into an exploratory process for accessing the larger picture, gaining a broader understanding, and accessing new possibilities..................................21

    3. How much of your life is made up of habitual behaviors?...23

    4. Inner observation, witnessing, and watching are the same thing. What are the benefits?...27

        A basic meditation practice..31

Bringing an intentional state of consciousness
into your everyday routines..32

5. Contemplation is an important part of a practice for
self-awareness, discovery, and personal growth..................33

Chapter Two: Uncovering the Fantasy Within

6. What is fantasy and how can I recognize it?........................43

7. Dependance on fantasy for a sense of comfort
and safety..59

8. How does fantasy influence procrastination?......................63

9. Two examples of fantasy scenarios with steps
for transforming them..64

Chapter Three: Understanding Internal Space

10. How can I better understand, create,
and make effective use of internal space?..........................68

Chapter Four: Compulsions and Engaging Your Inner Warrior

11. What is a compulsion and what can I do about it? 77

12. Transitioning compulsions back into conscious choices......81

A process for transitioning compulsions back into
conscious choices..104

13. What is my inner Warrior and how do I participate
with that part of me? 108

    Helpful steps for engaging your inner warrior..114

Chapter Five: Overcommitting Yourself Can Block Authentic Experience and Negatively Affect Your Overall Health

  14. The importance of having space between responsibilities and activities..118

  15. Familiarizing yourself with a conscious non-doing state.....................130

      Steps for transitioning from an over-committed state to a balanced experience..133

  16. Techniques for resolving anxiety when you are worried or overwhelmed..136

  17. Instructions for a walking meditation..137

  18. Instructions for a regenerative meditation..138

Chapter Six: Common Obstacles to Self-Awareness

  19. How can I recognize when I am personalizing?..141

      Steps for transitioning beyond the habit of personalizing..162

  20. What are personal boundaries?..165

      Steps for creating healthy boundaries..172

  21. What is drama and how does it get created?..173

The negative effects of drama..182

A process for overcoming patterns of drama..186

Chapter Seven: Confidence Matters

22. What is personal confidence?..190

23. How does a person build confidence?..195

24. What are some of the challenges that you may encounter while building confidence?..199

Chapter Eight: Comparison, Belief in Sameness, and Compliance

25. The act of comparison reinforces expectations of sameness..209

A process for discerning truth from fantasy, individuality, and boundaries between yourself and others..213

26. Understanding self-doubt and lack of confidence..217

Chapter Nine: An In-depth View of Anger and Judgment

27. Participation with judgment, anger, and fixed ideas is sometimes used to dominate and control others..220

28. Transformational steps for the aggressor..225

29. Transformational steps for the recipient of aggression 228

30. How to overcome self-judgment and deal with judgment coming from others while building inner strength and confidence 232

31. Understanding anger and the use of rules 236

32. The struggle between victimhood and anger based, dominant behavior created from the use of rules and judgment 240

    Steps for transitioning beyond victimhood and the role of dominance created from the use of judgment and anger 243

33. When you let go of judgment and engage your curiosity, understanding will be your reward 245

Chapter Ten: The Home Stretch

34. Acceptance vs desire for something else 249

35. Birthing yourself from a concept-based experience into the substance of life 250

36. A bridge well-built – Writing your own conclusion 257

Biography 262

Introduction

After writing my first book, The Missing Link – *A spiritual guide for understanding addictive behaviors*, I realized that a second book was needed which could serve as a step-by-step guide/workbook to help people learn how to effectively process while accessing a deep understanding of themselves and life. The first book gave an overview of the many unconscious compulsive behaviors that interfere with a person's ability to fully function within the quality of life.[1] This book teaches a process for transcending many inner struggles through self-awareness.   Throughout this participatory workbook, you will be given support as you work your way through a step-by-step process for realizing how to utilize observation, curiosity, surrender, discovery, and contemplation. You will also be shown how to create healthy boundaries, apply new understanding, and honestly participate with purpose. This book is intended to assist you to recognize your long-standing, unconscious conditioning while helping you to discern the difference between unhealthy imagination and the truthfulness that comes through a present state of awareness. This book also addresses the conditioned, concept-based mind and how it becomes an obstacle to a present state of awareness when it is dominant. Concept-based thinking occurs when a person gets stuck in set ideas, surface level thinking, black and white processing,

---

[1] * "The Missing Link" broke down numerous patterns of behavior and beliefs at the foundation of compulsive experience to bring about a cohesive understanding of the limitations of fragmented processing. It also offered an understanding of the tools and skills needed to effectively navigate diverse challenges, to access wisdom, and to create change.

reactions, and faulty beliefs. This can be a barrier to accessing a deep experiential level within the self, and it can also influence habitual emotional reactions. When a person is present and aware, the experiential self leads the mind, instead of the mind leading the experience. Throughout this book, you will be shown the option of choice in ways that you may not have previously recognized. You will also be shown how to apply new understanding in your daily life for the purpose of discovery and change. Once this is accomplished, you will be far less distracted by habitual approaches, reactions, unhealthy imagination, drama-based stories, judgments, fragmented processing, etc. As you practice, the step-by-step guidance will gradually lead you to a deep experiential level of self. Along with this comes the realization of presence, inner peace, and freedom. This is the level of consciousness from which wisdom and insight arise.

When you embrace this guidance and apply it beyond the surface level of the mind, you will have a chance to discover what it means to live in the moment more often. When you are present in the moment, you are living in the true substance of life.

Through recognition of the truth within many of your behaviors, you will naturally reconfigure the way that you interact with yourself, other people, and relate to your everyday circumstances and possibilities. All of what is being offered can be applied to your life in general and to your personal obstacles and struggles, thereby giving you the option to transition out of suffering into a more conscious experience. An ongoing commitment is required on your part so that in-depth lasting change can take place. Once this practice becomes a regular part of your functioning, then understanding, peacefulness, and fulfillment can be more frequently experienced. This process provides a bridge from basic ideas to understanding, to receptive participation, to change, and to a sense of freedom which can be realized in all areas of life. A pathway to a deep experiential level of understanding of yourself and life is possible through full participation with the guidance contained within this book.

It is my hope that the guidance will lead individuals into an experience of greater self-awareness beyond suffering. The possibility for self-awareness and inner freedom exists within all human beings.

All that is contained in this book has come from my own lifelong experience of seeking, discovery, learning, and helping others to grow and heal. My own practices for self-awareness began at a young age. This book includes the wisdom that has come through profound spiritual experiences as well as ongoing self-inquiry.

The most influential spiritual experience took place when I was 21 years old, was in extreme pain for two days, temporarily left my body, and transcended into the light of creation – Divine consciousness. This experience brought about the realization that there is more to life than what most people perceive. There is a pure consciousness that connects every person and everything in this world. That experience led me on a spiritual quest. I had many questions. How and why did that happen? Why did I feel changed by it? What significance would it have for me in my ongoing life? How could I access the full experience of oneness on a daily basis? Would I find it in a particular religion or through a spiritual practice? My spiritual quest spanned over many years, and the answers gradually unfolded.

Much insight, personal growth, and wisdom also came from an inquiry into painful challenges that were imprinted by a traumatic upbringing. In the household there were alcohol, drama, and rage addictions along with co-dependent behaviors. I was blessed to have never had any challenges with alcohol or substance abuse. My preference has been to be in a natural state.

Within the family environment, individuality, which included authentic needs, perspectives, feelings, goals, and personal confidence was not allowed. Any expression of individual truth was forbidden, unless by chance, it fit a rule-based narrative. Conformity to the rules, whether known or unknown was expected. Hence, fear was the most consistent underlying state within the family. This resulted in ongoing confusion and emptiness that had no known solution. Only imagined solutions could come through the fantasy within drama. Drama addiction was imprinted on all family members. Because of the need to predict the unspoken parental expectations, I developed a fine-tuned focus and acute intuitive abilities. The discomforts from that history led to a deep inquiry of myself and all of life. Thus began the practice of self-awareness. The multi-leveled focus and intuition that I developed in childhood have been valuable in my self-awareness practice for healing, growth, and the realization of presence. The discomforts served as a doorway for accessing wisdom and transformation.

For me, there was confusion about how to be a *normal* human being – like the other people I witnessed around me on a daily basis. Behind the suffering within me there existed a subtle curiosity along with a need to understand what was missing in myself and my ability to process life. That curiosity drew my attention inside of myself to watch and question what was actually happening and why. The answers and understanding came to me gradually over the years though vigilant inner inquiry and contemplation. Eventually many pieces of truth emerged and transitioned me into a place of harmony and freedom. I am truly blessed, and it has been my life's work to assist others to realize the truths within themselves that will transition them into greater presence – the substance of life – into freedom and peace.

Through my professional practice, South Shore Natural Healing, I have assisted thousands of people for over three decades with their personal journeys toward self-discovery, emotional/spiritual growth, healing, and greater freedom. At times, they have unknowingly taught me as much as I taught them. Sometimes when you see for others, you are seeing for yourself as well. The profound mystical experiences have been many throughout my life. They established and continue to reinforce an awareness of the Divine in all of life.

Most of what is in this book was created while in a state of pure presence. Some of it was written during a time when I was suffering from a severe concussion from a car accident. During that time, I could mostly only sit or lie down while surrendering to the pure essence of the moment, thereby letting go of the conditioned mind. I realized that the substance of experience was profound when the routine mind was really out of the way. The intensity of this went on for months and gradually resolved over a two-year period. Almost everything felt challenging. However, one day early on I decided to see if I could write, and it flowed with grace.

At that time, I was not able to function normally in my daily routines. Walking half a block or cooking food was extremely difficult. If I tried to drive 5 minutes down the road to get food, the bombardment of stimuli made me feel as if I was in an overwhelming battle – at war with my own brain. I had been diagnosed by a physician's assistant who recommended a neurologist. She said that he would be the one to explain what was happening and could tell me what I should or should not be doing. However, further medical assistance was not available for what seemed like an eternity due the six-week wait time required by each doctor's office that I called. Undeterred, I finally did manage to make an appointment with a local neurologist within three weeks. I was told on arrival that it was a mistake – that the receptionist should have never scheduled me. As I pleaded for help, I was shown the door. The doctor would not see me, so I was left on my own to try to figure out what was happening. I had to figure out how I could best help myself. It was also quite challenging because most people could not see or perceive the extent of my limitations. I could still speak and be understood, and there were no physical signs of injury, but my brain would just shut down after 20 to 45 minutes of what had previously appeared to be normal functioning. I did eventually find some medical help through physical therapy, a chiropractor who practiced applied kinesiology, and an exceptionally kind neurologist from out of town. The internet also proved to be a great resource for accessing information and understanding. Daily meditation was invaluable at that time.

My history of knowing how to be present also served me well at that time. I had no choice in the matter anyway. I continued to write every day for very short intervals and then meditated and rested at length. It is one thing to write from a place of presence when you know that your mind is available to you. You can utilize it to process layers of ideas and possibilities. It is a different kind of experience when you know that it is not available for use in the typical manner. In this case, a deep level of contemplation takes place on a pure experiential level of functioning. A near complete rough draft of this book was written at that time. It is important to have an intellect; however, I had clear confirmation through direct experience that the mind alone provides a superficial level of functioning. There is a level of consciousness within all of us that is much deeper than the thinking mind. A sense of wholeness, understanding, and knowing occurs when the conditioned mind is out of the way.

Some of you may have previously experienced a writing style that required some contemplation before engaging with this book. If you have and you tried to read it in the same way that you would read a book with basic information or a straightforward narrative, it would have seemed difficult and rightly so. You may have experienced this struggle while attempting to read historical texts, philosophical writings, or poetry – for instance the Bhagavad-Gita, or work by Plato, Rumi, Shakespeare, Emerson, or even more recent offerings like Thomas Keating's books or *A Course in Miracles*. For in-depth understanding of these works, curiosity, a state of presence, and reflection are required. If you did not understand what was required for such reading you would have likely put it aside, felt as though it was not for you, or even felt defeated. A fixed mindset will not work for reading this type of writing.

When you are functioning in a mind-dominant state, devoid of curiosity, you will be present on a level of consciousness that identifies mainly through concepts, rules, known ideas, and either/or thinking. The psyche will associate what it sees with something that it already knows through comparison, historical understanding, projection of self-created rules, judgments, ideas of what should be, etc. These are all containers for readymade projections of what has already been. Association and identification in this way can bring about resistance to the present moment and the process of discovery. The mind alone will be pleased to imagine whole experiences through individual concepts. There are many books that have been created primary for a concept level of understanding and will fulfill a desire to accumulate intellectual information. Sometimes, that is what is needed, and at other times a person may need to go deeper.

The substance of life cannot be assimilated by the mind alone. The conditioned mind, by itself, perceives limited ideas, concepts, and basic understanding. It is a useful starting point. If you want to access the depth of life, you must be willing to be present at a level of depth within yourself – from a place of unobstructed receptivity. Curiosity and contemplation are most often essential for making discoveries, gaining new understanding, and transitioning into a level of deep experience so that any new realizations can be fully integrated into the subconscious.

When you learn how to access your subconscious and beyond, you will have the option to embark upon an avenue for discovery, understanding, fulfillment, or make changes anytime and anywhere. A familiar process for quick access to the subconscious to facilitate change is hypnosis. However, it can be more useful to learn how to access any level of your consciousness naturally and spontaneously on a regular basis and be your own creator. This book can teach you that.

So, why do so many people process life on a surface level? This occurs because many people are conditioned to take in life in a mind-dominant manner as well as look to the outside for understanding and wisdom rather than inside of themselves. Many factors have influenced this. Some of this is from societal and generational conditioning. Additionally, a fast pace of life keeps people running on the surface of experience while chasing after the next thing. This leaves little space to simply *be*. They often have an urgency to get away from their immediate experience so that they can go on to the next agenda and then the one after that and so on. Because of this fast pace, family connections and community relationships are often undervalued or not a priority. This adds to the deficit of deeper experience and authentic connection beyond the mind. Also, so many of the processes which kept people connected to the depth of life, for sustaining their place on this earth have been eliminated through instant accessibility to whatever they desire.

Many people choose to have someone else do many things for them where they would have otherwise been required to participate for themselves. Examples of this include traveling on foot to their destination, cooking, cleaning, organizing, sewing, wisdom-based storytelling, growing food, yardwork, house maintenance, solving problems as a MacGyver, as well as helping one another, deep listening, taking care of the elderly or those who are ill, and enjoying unplanned leisure time. Connections with the earth and between people are often not a priority as much as acquiring, achieving, competing, gossiping, and looking for temporary fulfillment. The point is that many participatory life supporting processes have the potential to bring a person into the depth of experience beyond the mind. They provide an opportunity to be present – they provide experiential understanding and an awareness of cause and effect. Additionally, space between activities is a very important part of this. Space itself invites reflection, curiosity, and contemplation. It is through these practices that a person accesses understanding and wisdom. If a balanced approach to life is not intact, a clear foundation of wisdom will not be intact. As a result, the mind is given free rein to dominate the consciousness.

Moreover, much of the world has transitioned into mind-based participation through technology. A large percentage of jobs are now technology based or require that a person use a computer for part of their work-related or personal requirements. Technology is a useful tool; however, when compulsive use replaces the opportunity for direct experience it becomes unhealthy. During free time many people have swapped out direct experience with themselves, others, or connection with the earth for obsessive surface level experience though the cell phone or computer. The mind is constantly being fed above all else and becomes like a parasite – constantly consuming. At this level of consumption, intimacy with others, self-awareness, and purposeful choices are diminished or nonexistent. All of this distracts a person from the experience of full presence and the deep inquiry that gives access to sustainable wisdom and deep knowing. For in-depth processing and understanding, it is necessary for a person to be experientially present while the mind takes up a secondary position. When you are experientially present, your focus is clean and steady. A state of presence brings with it an element of grace which permeates each experience as it unfolds. You are naturally fulfilled; you do not have to chase after anything. A full life experience can be realized and sustained through clear processing, self-awareness, presence, and conscious discernment of choices. The goal of this book is to assist you to discover how to consciously manage your life and be present within yourself and the substance of all that unfolds before you. You will be learning a new process which is your bridge to freedom.

If you can relate to this or have some curiosity, then this book will likely be of great value to you. When you apply the wisdom that is presented in this guide, you will have an opportunity to transition beyond your conditioned blueprint. Meaningful life changes and learning that go beyond the mind can occur for you.

The information contained herein is intended to be processed slowly through contemplation. Each section of the book builds upon the preceding one. If you have difficulty with a particular section, then move on from it for the time being. Give it some space, and then go back to it later. This book provides a broad understanding of the interconnectedness of many aspects of unconscious and conscious behavior. You will gain the most value from the book if you read it in its entirety.

Chapter One

Chapter One

Refocusing Your Lens

-1-

Building a bridge from basic ideas to discovery, in-depth understanding, and a new process

What if you had the chance to re-create your life – to start fresh – to be a creator instead of a passive participant – would that be something that you would like to embrace? What if you had the chance to live with purpose and meaning on a daily basis? Did you know that this possibility is available to you? It is something that can be realized when you learn to be consciously present with your thoughts, feelings, needs, and options. It is then that you can access a clearer understanding of life and make ongoing purposeful choices. A large percentage of people in the world function unconsciously in habitual patterns and compulsive streams of thought. They are held captive by the beliefs and unconscious historical records of the mind. They do not realize that this is happening.

The goal of this book is to teach you to see and understand yourself with greater clarity and to be more presence and more self-awareness, so that you can make conscious choices, thereby creating a life with greater purpose and fulfillment. For change to occur, you must make choices for yourself based on recognition of real facts, available options, and truth-based experience rather than desire or fantasy. You also must be committed to participating with an ever-changing understanding of yourself and life. If you cannot honestly perceive the truth of yourself and your situations in the moment, then the creative potential for your experiences will be limited. Through conscious, curious direct participation, contemplation, and new realizations you can learn to decipher the truth of your approaches, beliefs, behaviors, obstacles, and options. As you gain a greater understanding, it will be necessary for you to apply your realizations for the purpose of challenging your set ways, to make ongoing discoveries, to learn, and to create a new reality. For this to happen, you must mindfully recognize and walk through your reactions, fears, and resistance as you participate in each step or choice. As you develop greater awareness in your life, your depth of participation will increase, and you will have a greater sense of trust for life. You will also sleep better, be more courageous, and have more understanding and compassion toward yourself and others. Through this process, you will have to deal with many learned behaviors and beliefs that have created personal limitations, suffering, chaos, and illusionary states.

When the lives of individuals are driven by unconscious reactions to their own histories, self-created stories, and skewed beliefs – they will struggle. If a person does not know how to look within to gain clarity about the self, they will most often look for answers or a sense of wholeness from people and situations on the outside. If your primary source of fulfillment for personal needs and validation is sought through other people or situations, then you will not be in charge of your own life. Manifestation and personal growth will happen by chance. This develops a dependency on others and a powerlessness within the self, which will lead to behaviors such as judgment, competition, apathy, envy, resentment, helplessness, anger, depression, struggle, and more. Another person cannot create growth or progress in your life for you. This occurs through direct experience and conscious participation with all facets of life. You must seek to understand your own behaviors and take responsibility for your personal choices. You might be asking, "How can I step out of my own inner struggles, my perceived limitations, personal chaos, and suffering? What am I doing that limits my discovery process?"

When understanding or solutions are needed for a particular struggle, you must utilize curiosity while looking inside of yourself more than you look outside. When you witness the processes of your mind and imagination alongside present-moment facts with an open-ended curiosity, then insight, understanding, and wisdom will naturally come. Curiosity is a receptive, inviting state. Once you gain some familiarity with a process of inner witnessing and know how to access understanding, you will be more trusting and motivated to seek answers through participation from within the unknown. This simply means that you accept that there is always more to know than what you think you already know. This awareness is needed for taking steps toward renewal, discovery, and change. Participation in one step will lead to the next step and the next. This is essential for creating the life that you want.

When in a state of suffering or challenge, sometimes a person will mistake their initial understanding of a situation for the total solution. If a person stops at the concept level of understanding, they will feel temporary relief, but then their stagnant circumstances will bring continued disappointment and struggle. The basic understanding of any experience gives you a starting point and then, as you contemplate, a first step becomes apparent in an ongoing process. There will likely be many more steps to make and discoveries that come from your participation in each choice or step. Think of the process as an exploratory, experiential, ongoing adventure that cannot be contained. The mind will consistently attempt to convince you that it knows the whole story before you live it. This is how it holds you captive in unconscious limited, closed-off, surface-level thinking. This limited process can most easily be understood when we look at our long established, unconscious ways of relating to set ideas, labels, and traditional beliefs.

-2-

How do set ideas, labels, and fantasy-based ideas create struggle, limitation, and suffering?

When habitually applied, the limited ideas that are suggested through labels and traditionally held beliefs can lead to distorted perceptions of people and situations. When these beliefs are accepted at face value, they can limit exploration and discovery, thereby limiting a person's receptivity to ongoing choices. Labels and set ideas can also create the illusion of predictability. People often allow the assumed rules and ideas associated with the label to make absolute decisions for them. All ideas are meant to provide a starting point – not a whole experience. They are meant to lead you into an open-ended process with the potential for many realizations and possible choices. The passive suggestions and basic ideas contained within labels will relay general, limited, surface representations about possibilities. If any limited interpretation replaces the discovery process involving a person or situation, it is likely that it will eventually lead to a struggle. The struggle may include judgment, personalization, comparison, competition, disappointment, perceptions of delegitimized value or inflated false value of a person, situation, talent, skill, or perception. This can also stunt the learning process and the ways in which people share.

For example, set ideas about race, spiritual beliefs, or economic status can create perceptions of inferiority or superiority, thereby creating limitations for the one who believes them. This can apply whether you are thinking about someone else, thinking about yourself, or when someone else is thinking about you. The negative effects most often come about from an unconscious, instead of a conscious, interpretation of the label or concept. I will emphasize – the label is not the problem by itself; it is the interpretation of the label that poses the problem. Every label carries an accumulation of beliefs that have been interwoven with it over time.

For instance, a person from a family of long-standing wealth might carry an inherited belief that people with money have greater intelligence, better values, and more human worth than someone who has fewer financial resources. Whereas someone who comes from poverty might carry an inherited belief that if someone is wealthy, they are likely to abuse their power, be arrogant, and mistreat other people. At either end of these hypothetical examples, a person would be engaging in a set of judgmental ideas which would also act as a personal barrier. Once these barriers are set in place, authentic participation for understanding and discovery of possibilities will be decreased or eliminated.

People sometimes unconsciously define a whole person's identity through a label when it relates to another person's religious beliefs. This occurs when set judgmental ideas have been infused into the labels. For instance, when such ideas are applied through a label, a Jewish person may be seen as one of those people who knocks on your door to preach religion; a Christian might be referred to a one of those born-again types; Muslim people have been referred to as those who want to harm others; people who identify as spiritual may be seen as those New Ager types. The individuality of each human being is lost to the perceiver when this type of thinking takes place. When a person is seduced by the simplicity of a definition or concept, the mind has hijacked them from the possibility of curiosity, contemplation, and discovery through direct participation with the intimacy of life. A concept-laden approach serves to dehumanize others. When you participate to discover, then sharing from within the depth of experience can bring understanding, and new possibilities among people.

Confusion and struggle can also occur in professional relationships. When a person relates through a template of what they think the professional is offering based on a label, set idea, or title rather than through an openness to discover individual abilities and true value, it becomes more difficult to gauge what is useful for a specific situation or not. For instance, someone might base an attorney's capabilities on the school where they studied rather than considering their actual skills and history of success. Maybe one attorney who has a natural affinity for the profession studied at the University of Mississippi, while someone else who does not have an innate talent for the profession studied at Yale. Even though the person who studied at the University of Mississippi was recommended as a superb attorney, someone who is seduced by the historical suggestions that are connected to the label Yale, may not make the best choice for their needs.

Sometimes people use single words or ideas that have been infused with their personal judgment to suggest a person's entire identity. They only see the person through the projection of a positive or negative judgment. When someone is reduced to inferior or inflated to superior through a description or idea of something, then their human experience is dismissed and replaced with the illusion of something that appears to be controllable. They are reduced to something that has no life – a basic idea. Some statements that reduce people in this way include the following: "That person says so little, they must not be very smart." "That woman drives so fast – she must be crazy." I've heard that person talk about everything under the sun – she is a literal genius. That man is so skinny – he is a death trap." "That person does not speak like other people – there is something wrong with them." "That woman is so gorgeous – she could get any man that she would ever want." "I've never known that person to work – they are a slacker." "That healer is so great – everybody needs to see him." All these perceptions have the potential to create a conceptual trap.

Additionally, individuals sometimes identify with one another through traditional labels such as mother, father, wife, husband, daughter, son, lover, girlfriend, boyfriend, etc. The expectations that are suggested within the historical use of the label can become an instrument of sabotage and a source of personalization between people. They do not allow for the discovery or true understanding between individual people. How often have you heard yourself or another person comment that their husband, wife, girlfriend, boyfriend should be a certain way that is based on some ideal perceptions that are suggested by the label. Some examples of this are: a mother should always understand her children; a mother should be there for her sons and daughters at any age; a father should always provide well for his family; a brother should be there to help; a sister should be available when you need her. People will do what is within their capacity based on learned behaviors or natural abilities. When someone is misled by infused ideals within a title, the lenses with which they process their choices will be black and white. This is a conceptual, superficial mind-base paradigm. If you put the labels aside and allow yourself to perceive the other person as a unique individual, through a state of curiosity, you will likely make discoveries and experience some degree of understanding that would not have been otherwise accessible. This means that you will have to let go of the fantasy and see each person as they are. When you perceive everyone as individual people, without a label or set idea, this invites the possibility of sharing more authentically from within the essence of the moment. It brings the possibility of honest interaction and the discovery of real options for authentic connection, navigation of differences, respect for individuality, and appropriate boundaries.

The ideas within traditional practices also have the potential to lead a person into unconscious habitual choices which may not fit for their true preferences or needs. Christmas is a good example of this. How many times have you heard yourself or someone else say, "I really dislike buying Christmas gifts and going into debt?" Yet it is done anyway. Or someone else might comment, "I really wish that I could just stay home at Christmas. I can't stand all the planning, running around, and family drama." Yet you or they do it anyway. Someone else might comment about a desire to go away for a holiday instead of participating in the routine activity, yet they do not do it. In these types of situations, people develop a relationship with self-created rules around the habitual holiday experience instead of choosing according to their true preferences.

In the next example the ideas from within a story are believed to represent a complete picture for the person reading it. When choices are made from limited beliefs, they can have consequences on the person's life.

For instance, let's say that as a result of reading a story, a man developed an interest in living on a tropical island. Based on the information in the story, he believed that it would be a perfect place for him to live. *The fantasy of living on an island felt fulfilling and complete*. However, no real inquiries with real people occurred. No research into the availability of jobs or standard of living in the desired location was done. The only inquiry made was for temporary lodging. With minimal planning, the man sold all his belongings and moved to the island with enough money to live on for six months. Once he arrived there, he moved into a bungalow. He had a lot of time off which was great, but there was no work. He was not well received by the locals, and he could not find a way to make it work for him. He realized through participating that maybe it wasn't the right choice, and he moved back home. At that point he had the realization that direct experience is different than what he may have concluded from an idea or elaboration on a story that was fabricated in his mind.

Perhaps it would have been beneficial for this person to have done some research and taken some prior exploratory trips to the location. In this way, he could have explored various situations to discern the availability options for a successful transition. People often try to totally decide things before they have any direct experience of a situation. This is because they believe what's in their mind. They do not realize or have familiarity with the value of discovery. A mind-based approach may initially appear to be more desirable and easier. However, it is more fantasy-driven than fact based which only brings the illusion of predictability and safety. When you believe that the idea is the same as having an experience, then you are taking a path that is likely to be fraught with disappointment and struggle.

Some people will go as far as to reject the discoveries of an experience when they are different than an imagined scenario. They may feel wronged, refuse to

Transitioning Beyond Your Conditioned Blueprint

consider the experience as natural, and feel like a victim. In that case, there will be resentment, distrust of life, and an inability to understand the value of discovery or the difference between truth and fantasy. This is an unconscious, damaging habit. Through curiosity, direct experience, and self-inquiry, a person can learn how to recognize when and how their participation with labels, set ideas, and their imagination is harming them or holding them back from living life more fully. The choice to follow ready-made ideas and imagination is most often the problem, not the experience.

Do you recognize any of what has been described from this section in your own behavior? Describe your experience in detail.

_____
_____
_____
_____
_____
_____
_____
_____
_____
_____
_____
_____
_____
_____
_____
_____
_____
_____
_____
_____

Now that you have identified a limiting practice, can you put aside the use of the label, set idea, traditional practice, or fantasy-based ideas? Can you approach your experience with curiosity and direct inquiry to discover the uniqueness of each person and situation? This means that you are open to discover something more beyond what you think you already know. You might ask yourself some of the following questions. Is my perception long-standing, or has it come from a discovery process? What are my beliefs in relation to this choice? Am I limited by those beliefs? Am I comfortable with them? Do I have resistance toward inquiry and discovery? Am I assuming something from the basis of a set idea rather than direct experience? Am I attached to a limited idea about a person or situation? Does this idea or belief require that I pretend in any way? If so, how does it feel to pretend?

Write down all that you have discovered.

Transitioning Beyond Your Conditioned Blueprint

Now, ask yourself: Am I aware of other alternate options or avenues for exploration? What prevents me from exploring or choosing differently? Can I identify a first step for participation in a process to discover something more beyond what my ideas or experiences have been?

Write down your discoveries.

Susan V. Kippen

Labels and set ideas will not give access to the full substance or value of an experience. They are limited by the suggestions that are interwoven into them. When a person lets a label define an experience for them, they have unconsciously given away an opportunity to participate directly, discover, and negotiate the possibilities within the natural unfolding reality. They have swapped an opportunity of exploration and presence for a fantasy. The substance of experience can only be realized through direct participation.

Perceptions of conceptual containment are compulsively identified with and unconsciously utilized within the world over. They are reinforced through shared habitual choices, projections, and interactions between people and situations.

Steps for transitioning from a basic idea into an exploratory process for accessing the larger picture, gaining a broader understanding, and accessing new possibilities is as follows.

1. You must recognize that the idea is the starting point. Your participation with this is a habit that was learned at some point in your life. You can choose and discover something more. The nature of a healthy life is one of continuous learning.

Transitioning Beyond Your Conditioned Blueprint

2. For increased discovery, you must engage your curiosity. Curiosity creates a space of receptivity within you. It invites more than what you already know through an open-ended invitation and state of surrender. You can create a receptive opening within by asking yourself a question. Some example questions might be, "What am I getting out of the attachment to this idea? How do I feel when I am actively engaged with it? Does it lead me into a state of limited thinking or judgment toward myself or another person?" Focus on one question at a time while allowing yourself to be still and present. Continue to ask questions until you feel that it is enough.
3. When you are seeking to discover, your mind may try to distract you with a story, judgment, resistance, analysis, or something else. The mind likes to keep familiar practices intact. If this happens simply acknowledge it, and then bring your focus back to a curious state while staying open to discover something new.
4. When new thoughts or insights come to you, contemplate them. As you do this, you will be inviting in-depth understanding. Also, you will likely perceive new choices.
5. Once you gain a broader understanding and see new possibilities for direct participation, know that you must apply this to your experience. This is how you gain true knowing. This knowing will vary from situation to situation. Every situation has the potential to teach you something new.
6. When deciding how to proceed, it is helpful to know that you only need to decide one step at a time. Each step that you take will help you to see the next step more clearly.
7. If your mind gets in the way by trying to predict an outcome, ignore it. Know that predictability is not possible in many situations. The experience itself will reveal the reality.
8. Predictability is often an illusion of the mind and an irrational habit. Conscious interruption of this must take place by simply witnessing it or implementing a new practice of curiosity and participation within the unknown.

9. Keep asking other people as well as yourself new questions and continue participating to discover.

-3-

How much of your life is made up of habitual behaviors?

Human beings are habitual by nature. By the time most behaviors become habitual, they are more or less unconscious. Everything that you do habitually was learned by doing it over and over many times. Each habit may have started from any number of influences such as an interest, a belief, a need, a passion, a reaction to a hurtful experience, a desire to escape pain, the need for safety or survival, etc. Routines are similar to habits, but they make use of a higher degree of conscious intention and attention. Some routines are essential for a person's health and well-being. The more present the person is, the greater the likelihood will be that he or she makes conscious choices.

Most people start their day with a routine such as taking a shower, having something hot to drink, exercising, reading, meditating, or something else. There will be many other routines throughout the day. For example, you must eat to stay alive, wear clothes to maintain warmth when it is cold, drink water when you are thirsty, sleep when you are tired, participate with other people to access understanding and have a source of community, work to maintain an income, etc. Some other healthy routines include working reasonable hours, eating regular meals, taking time to relax, engaging in purposeful use of the internet, and using your creativity when problem solving. These are all supportive routines. Some familiar healthy supportive routines which are most often associated with conscious choices are meditation, service to others, prayer, reasonable exercise, healthy eating, and purposeful sharing. Every day your personal needs, the details of your circumstances, and situations will be varied. Therefore, it is important to practice participating consciously with all routines. You can decide through reflection and discernment whether a routine will be a healthy or unhealthy fit for your needs and circumstances. If the routines become unconscious, then there is a likelihood that they could fluctuate between a healthy routine and an unhealthy habit. Also, when faulty beliefs infiltrate healthy routines, there is a likelihood that they will become unconscious habits.

Faulty beliefs will limit the way that you process your choices. For example, if a person becomes attached to relaxing and feeling good, they may avoid the discomfort which sometimes comes from the need to apply effort and progress in a career. Yet, on the other hand, if a person continues to climb the ladder of success while feeling the need to consistently prove their own worth, they may lose sight of the balance needed between the areas of work and family life. In another instance, if a person loves to read novels and over overidentifies with the fulfillment that comes through the fantasy of the story, the time spent reading could become excessive. Additionally, when a person believes that they must have all the answers to life, they may become attached to getting information from books rather than through the discovery which comes with direct experience. Therefore, make it a point to consciously consider whether a choice is fitting each time that you make it. If someone overidentifies with a healthy routine, it could develop into an all-consuming habit and prevent the person from perceiving the larger picture and maintaining overall balance.

If your life becomes too habitual you may lose your passion, be led by compulsions, feel like something is missing, or you may become depressed. This is when a person may no longer perceive or realize that they have choices. You might ask yourself, "What other influences come into play when a routine transitions into an unconscious habit?"

The root cause comes from a loss of the innocent curiosity that is present with everyone at birth. Curiosity is a very natural open-ended receptive state which invites the unknown and the larger picture from the ongoing substance of life. If there is no curiosity, there is little discovery or new learning. Curiosity also creates an internal pause that makes room for you to witness and contemplate, and it helps you to access wisdom from the depths of your experiences and integrate it. The combined use of curiosity and contemplation provides a relaxed, graceful means of weighing out your experiences for discerning value, individuality, responsibilities, accessing understanding, and more. Instead of predicting an outcome, curiosity, witnessing, and contemplation most often bring about access to understanding. There is an openness to discover rather than to get stuck, analyze, judge, assume, or make up stories. Without this present moment process, a person would be prone to a life of black and white perceptions, along with all the accompanied limitations and struggles that come with participation in limited set beliefs.

Unconscious, habitual behaviors come in many forms. Do you find yourself being led by your emotional reactions? These are habitual re-enactments of the past. Are you aware of any set ideas that routinely make decisions for you? These come from closed beliefs. Do you have resistance toward making new discoveries and choices? This comes from a belief that you are your history. Rigid ideas often have judgments intertwined in them along with blame and guilt, or shame toward the self and others for noncompliance. This approach can lead to impatience, self-doubt, self-righteousness, feelings of competition, displaced responsibility, and resistance toward anything that is different or authentic. Most people have many habitual, unconscious approaches that automatically decide things for them.

As you reflect, can you identify a familiar habitual routine or behavior in your life? To practice some self-inquiry, activate a curious state. To create this state, you can begin by recognizing any areas of your life where you are routinely curious. In a situation when another person is teaching you something, it is likely that you will be in a state of curiosity, and you will be present. Or, if someone is telling a story, your curiosity is active when you want to hear more. This is also common when you are trying to understand someone who speaks with an accent or in any situation where you are observing and asking yourself, "What is happening here?" As you recall any such experience see if you can replicate that state and transfer it into this practice now.

Remember that curiosity has a receptive, relaxed quality. Put your focus and active curiosity on the habitual behavior that you have identified. Next, observe it to see if you discover anything new. You could also ask yourself a question about your habitual routine or behavior. Example questions are as follows: Does it serve me in any purposeful way? If not, what am I getting out of it? Do I find comfort in it? Does it distract me from anything, compromise my relationships, or overall life? Does it affect other people in a harmful way? Does it consume my free time? Do I have any resistance to change it? Let your questions sit one at a time in the space of curiosity. Be patient with each one of them. If no insight or answers come to you, then temporarily step away from it. Go back and check on

Transitioning Beyond Your Conditioned Blueprint

it periodically. An insight may come quickly or at any time within hours or days. There is no timeframe and there is no force.

Write down your discoveries.

When you find yourself stuck or struggling in day-to-day life, practice using your curiosity. The more that you engage your curiosity, the more that you will understand yourself, other people, and your situations.

-4-

Inner observing, witnessing, and watching are the same thing. What are the broad benefits?

At first, it is important to become very familiar with the practice of looking inward to identify the basics of your own inner experience. If you practice observing your thoughts, feelings, and beliefs regularly, it will become more natural for you. Observing is the same as witnessing or watching. Initially, it is best to do this in a solo manner. If you are interacting with another person and attempting to do this, it becomes more complex. Because of the need to negotiate between your own experience, that of another person, and of shared interactions, it would likely be hard to maintain a steady conscious focus. Instead, you will probably find yourself feeling distracted and stressed. Because of this, keep this step within your private practice until you have some familiarity with the process. At some point, you will be able to focus on multiple levels simultaneously.

As discoveries and insights come through self-observation, you will gain a deeper understanding of your beliefs, approaches, and behaviors. You will also see where there is a need to make change or discover something else. Some contemplation may be needed as insights arise. It is important to know that contemplation is different than analyzing. Contemplation is an experiential process of being totally present, curious, and asking yourself open-ended questions while considering all possibilities, discoveries, and insights. Analyzing is the practice of dissecting to categorize while seeing a relationship between the parts. It is more mind centered. When witnessing, you are not separate from the curiosity. You are the witnesser, the curiosity, and the space. If this does not make

Transitioning Beyond Your Conditioned Blueprint

sense to you now, no worries, it will make sense later. Through this process, you can access a broad understanding of yourself and all aspects of life. The practice of witnessing can be applied at any time throughout the day. The more you observe inwardly, the more discoveries you will make. You may be surprised to realize how much of your life has been unconscious.

As you proceed, your mind may fight you when you seek to see what is actually going on with your patterns of thinking, feeling, reacting, and believing. You may find yourself becoming impatient or distracted by a story. When this happens acknowledge it, then pull your focus back into the position of the watcher.

If you find yourself stuck interacting in habitual ways, you can use open-ended questions as a tool to interrupt the habit or pattern. This also creates a pause and engages your curiosity. Use your inquiry in the way that you would if you were seeking to understand a friend or creatively solve a problem. When you ask the question, let it sit in the space of curiosity, and see if something or nothing comes to you. You will be inviting insight, but you will not be grasping for anything. Example questions might be, "What is this about? What am I trying to accomplish? What beliefs underlie this behavior? What is this limited approach doing for me?"

If any resistance arises, then let it sit there along with your question. They can exist together. Observe both while in a state of active curiosity. Let go of the need to force an outcome. Greater clarity and understanding will arise either gradually or all at once. As you discover more details or pieces of truth, this will ignite more motivation to continue your inquiry. This is because your psyche is getting rewarded. Maintain the curiosity with whatever you see or don't see and keep going. As you develop the ability to create more space through witnessing, deep understanding will naturally follow along with more surrender and more peace. It will also lead to a natural automatic process of contemplation. Contemplation or reflection will lead a person to a place where they can access a broader view of any experience. True contemplation is free of judgment. It brings greater understanding as well as access to more options. Once you make a discovery, contemplate it so that it becomes anchored on a deep level of consciousness. This is essential; otherwise, it could just slip through the mind. It is also important that you participate with any newly discovered options in real life circumstances so that you have a direct experience of their value, purpose, and meaning.

Susan V. Kippen

Sometimes people are afraid to participate in a new way for various reasons such as an unfamiliarity with the process, a long-standing habit of self-doubt, fear of making a mistake, complacency with what is familiar, fear of being wrong, rejected, or judged, etc.

For example, you may recall people sharing their passion and excitement about getting a new perfect job and feeling happy with the idea of what they imagined the circumstances would be. At the start, they were able to be present while giving each moment the best of what they had to offer. The newness of the job encouraged their natural curiosity and an openness to observe, discover, and learn more. However, when they were challenged by unforeseen circumstances, they responded with judgment, resistance, and blame. Their historical programming got activated and distracted them from recognizing and embracing the best of what was available in the new situation. They soon regressed into their long-standing, unconscious habits while projecting more problems and ending up in a familiar, cyclical struggle. Their ability to observe and be curious got shut down by their own conditioning. They perceived the problem to be with the job, when in reality they were simply looking through their own familiar lenses and reacting in habitual ways. The opportunity for a direct experience in something new was lost through an unconscious association with long-standing beliefs. Inner witnessing and inquiry are necessary for discerning one's historical beliefs, behaviors, and limitations as well as for discovering any new potential.

The longer a habit is in place, the more unconscious it will become. Sometimes people become so entrenched in limiting habits and fear of change that they leave relationships, sabotage their jobs, and in the extreme, have nervous breakdowns. Resistance to discovery and change is often the problem. However, there is purpose and learning in every type of scenario. People continue with their unconscious patterns because they don't understand what is happening or how to make it better. If they do nothing to create change the result is long term suffering. This is where curiosity and inner witnessing can be beneficial. Once a person understands what is happening and embraces new possibilities, they can make purposeful changes to remedy the problems. As a person proceeds, some discomfort will occur as habits or obstacles are challenged. This is a natural part of the learning process. It must simply be accepted as a part of life.

Transitioning Beyond Your Conditioned Blueprint

Self-awareness is crucial for healing and personal growth. To change, a person must first recognize that something about them has been unconscious, accept this, take responsibility, be present, realize new options, take a first step toward change and make a commitment to participate with each new realization.

At first, the practice of self-awareness is a tool that will help you to have greater clarity, discernment, confidence, trust, and fulfillment as you participate in your everyday life. Eventually, it becomes a natural way of being. Continued practice brings freedom from the enslavement of unconsciousness.

When you bring this practice to the outside world, it will become more challenging. It will take a bit more effort and self-discipline to implement. Your personal beliefs, reactions, defense mechanisms, desires, and internal stories will sometimes be present in your exchanges with other people, as will theirs with you. The lines of individual responsibility will be blurred until you begin to differentiate your own behaviors from those of others through a truth-based, non-judgmental approach. In order to learn how to recognize misconceptions, faulty beliefs, and obstacles in others, you will need to learn how to recognize and negotiate such tendencies in yourself first. Initially, it is best to simply witness yourself as you participate with another person. Be aware of your reactions, roles, or past memories and the way they interject stories, resistance, and judgments into present situations. As you participate with this awareness, you will make discoveries and learn to create internal personal boundaries.

You can practice periodically throughout the day on your own or with others. Other people need not know what you are doing internally. All you need to do is create a commitment to occasionally notice your internal habits, themes, stories, thoughts, and emotions. When you do this, you are meeting the moment as it exists without jumping into pieces of fantasy. When considering choices, it is important to look at your authentic feelings and needs in relation to the real details of your overall situation.

This is a process, and a commitment to making ongoing discoveries is the key to your success. Meditation is another way to develop the skills that support presence. You might want to start with a meditation practice and then gradually integrate it into your day-to-day experiences. Once you learn how to witness and make use of internal space, you have the foundation for bringing it into daily life. Meditation is also a useful practice for clearing yourself on an energetic level.

A basic meditation practice

Meditation historically has been used for clearing the mind and developing an ability to be present. It usually involves being physically still and maintaining a clear focus while surrendering and watching, but not engaging with your thoughts, habitual inner experience, or reactions. Once you become well practiced, meditation can provide the foundation for being present in your daily life. This is not learned over night – it takes time – be patient.

The following is a basic meditation.

1. Find a quiet place to sit or lie down.
2. Close your eyes and focus your attention inward. It helps to initially put yourself in a state curiosity. This will help to open up some inner space. Once you become aware of this space, notice the expansive nature of it. This expansiveness has no agenda in it and no boundaries. This is presence. While in this present moment state you can notice whatever comes and goes. Let go of any attachment to or expectation of anything in particular.
3. Simply allow yourself to stay in the space of watching – like watching the clouds in the sky.
4. If any thoughts or emotions appear, refrain from engaging with or adding anything to them. Whatever appears will soon disappear, and then something else will show up. If you engage with ideas or feelings, the sense of watching and of space will close down and appear to be lost. This will occur if you add more ideas, a story, an argument, put yourself in a role, or in a state of resistance.
5. If you notice this happening, bring your focus back to the watching state. Every time you bring yourself back to a state of observation more internal space will naturally be created. You will also be learning what it is to surrender.
6. To surrender means to let go – you have no agenda. If you are simply watching, then this happens naturally. With surrender, the watching state

becomes a clean experiential state. It is a state of just being. This is a practice that you may eventually integrate into your everyday solo life and then shared experiences.

While meditation may be difficult at first, with practice it becomes easier. Stay committed and you will make progress. Forget about having a timeframe. If you become attached to a timeframe, you will more than likely become impatient, judge yourself and the process, create the illusion of failure, and give up. Instead, simply continue. As you continue to practice, you will realize that through witnessing, experiential understanding, and expanded seeing you will have more inner peace.

Bringing an intentional state of consciousness into your everyday routines

Wherever daily routines are already in place, you can practice being more present on an experiential level. This means that your mind is not taking you into some alternate imaginary experience. If you are cooking, pay attention to the food, the preparation, the smell, and the coming together of the ingredients. If you are vacuuming be present to notice what you are vacuuming, the motion of your body, and the change of details from room to room. When mowing the lawn, experience your relationship to the mower. Notice the smell of the grass, your body movements, how you maneuver the dips and level areas. Settle into the experience. Since the mind is most comfortable in a habitual state, it will likely try to resist a state of presence. You may notice some resistance toward full participation. You may notice stories sneaking into your mind. If that happens, just notice it, and bring yourself back to a witnessing state. Sometimes when you are not present, the mind will fill up your experience with a stream of thought that is fantasy based. When you are present, your experience will be clean and simple.

Another beneficial area of practice is when you are outdoors. Notice all the details that are around you whether you are sitting or walking. This would include what you see, hear, smell, sense, and feel. Do not associate anything you perceive with past experiences, likes or dislikes, etc.

Once you feel confident in your ability to be present – to observe yourself and your situation, it will be time to bring more contemplation into your present moment solo or shared experiences. Contemplation is your doorway for accessing a deeper experience of yourself and all of life.

-5-

Contemplation is an important part of a practice for self-awareness, discovery, and personal growth.

If you have limited experience with contemplation, you might be asking, "What is it, and how do I do it? Is it something that should be practiced separately from witnessing and curiosity?"

Contemplation is a process of bringing your thoughts or experiences into a place of deep introspection. Witnessing and curiosity are part of your contemplation process. Your mind, heart, and experiential self are actively receptive. When your goal is to contemplate an experience that rises from within you, you simply watch what is unfolding with curiosity, and open-ended consideration. You may want to ask an open-ended question during the experience. As you question, you remain receptive and considerate toward any possibilities that arise in your awareness. You are not attached to any specific detail or conclusion. You are receptive, not dependent. There is no attempt to possess anything. There is a state of open receptivity from which you may discover additional details, experience, understanding, possibilities – or nothing. There is no attempt to force anything. If you are not curious or if you are firmly attached to what you already know, this will shut the door for realizing more. To practice contemplation and curiosity you invite something, but you don't know what it is, and you are not expecting anything specific.

For instance, if you are experiencing a conflict or struggling, then by considering all the details of the entire experience, additional understanding and solutions may naturally emerge from within. When this happens, you have the option to consider the information. Through contemplation you are weighing details and options on mental and experiential levels at the same time. The mind

Transitioning Beyond Your Conditioned Blueprint

is not in a dominant position. You are trying on the insights rather than just thinking about them.

To practice this, first identify a habitual, limiting belief that keeps you stuck. Now, bring your focus inward and look at this belief with curiosity. Let the limiting belief sit in the space that is created from your open-ended curiosity. Remember curiosity is a receptive state. It invites what you do not already know. You do not need to force anything to happen. Insights and realizations naturally come from within this space of active curiosity. However, sometimes it helps to ask a question. You might ask, "What is true and untrue about this belief?" If any realizations appear, let yourself consider them. It's like trying them on. As you contemplate, the realizations that arise may stabilize into a place of deep knowing.

Practice this now, then describe your experience.

Susan V. Kippen

_____
_____
_____
_____
_____
_____
_____

Let's practice further by looking at some possible steps leading up to contemplation. To begin, bring your focus inward, and activate your curiosity. Then observe a long-standing personal belief or idea, concern, or obstacle along with any emotions that come with it. If additional beliefs or thoughts arise through your observation, then consider them too. If nothing comes, you could ask yourself a question about the belief, concern, etc. You could ask, "How have I been limited by this belief?" Then allow a space to open at the end of the question. That space will have an experiential quality to it – an aliveness. You can sit with it in the way that you would with a friend while seeking to understand one of their experiences. Imagine asking yourself a question in the way that you would ask your friend a question. In the same way that you would allow a space for them to find their own answer, allow that space for yourself. Refrain from letting your mind grasp for an answer. You are holding the space for yourself by maintaining an open-ended curiosity. You are present in a non-dominant manner – you are not urgently grasping for anything. You simply watch to see if anything comes in response to your question. Sometimes nothing comes in the moment, but it may come later. The intent is to be open for any insight, understanding, or anything else that may occur in your awareness. Your experience will have more substance than what the mind routinely offers. If your mind immediately goes to a routine reactive role or resistance toward the process, just observe the resistance or reaction. Resistance is made up of a judgment along with an active desire for something else. In this case, focus on the judgment or desire along with the curiosity and open-ended receptivity. If you can keep your focus intact, the resistance will likely fade. Then you can refocus on your open-ended question.

You might also ask yourself some practical questions like, "How did I arrive at that perception or belief? What is it doing for me? Does it provide value for me or not? Am I afraid to look at it? Am I afraid to break some self-made rules? Am I afraid to consider something new beyond my present belief? Is there something that I have not yet considered? What else might be required for more clarity? Are there any secondary beliefs contained within the first belief?

An example of a belief that may contain other beliefs would be a set idea that something is too difficult for you. The secondary belief could come from thinking that you are not smart enough or that you will fail if you try. If you discover a secondary belief, contemplate that one first and then transfer your focus back to the first one. Only ask yourself one question at a time. Be open and unattached when you ask yourself the questions.

Sometimes nothing comes. There can be no urgency or timeframe connected to your inquiries. When observing you may notice that your subconscious mind wants to continue to fight by bringing in more resistance, a judgment, a story, etc. In this case, shift your focus again to observe the struggle while questioning it. Once the struggle disappears, you can return your focus to the original idea, concern, obstacle, or belief and continue witnessing. Insights will often come along with a sense of expansion and feeling of peace. Continue to try on and weigh any insights that come to you on an experiential level through contemplation.

Do not try to force or add anything in a concrete way or go for a ride with a story. This will feed a mind dominant state, belief, or habit. A large part of what takes place in the mind and emotions is unconscious. Sometimes, when you start asking yourself questions, old stories will appear from the past that are somewhat relevant in the present. There may be a hidden belief in the past story that relates to the present. The mind loves to associate the essence of an experience from the past with something in the present. If you see this happening, simply acknowledge it, but do not become immersed in it. You could choose to contemplate the story to see if any insight comes about a belief that also relates to the present. The main thing is to keep practicing. Consider all insights. With experience, this new process can be slowly transitioned into your everyday situations. Many opportunities for practice will occur or be triggered in your day-to-day situations as reactions arise within you.

Where reactions occur, you will often find yourself asking, "Why am I doing that?" The reasons why are recorded somewhere in your history. Most reactions are a reenactment of something that occurred in the past. To understand what is happening, you may have to explore layers of beliefs and walk through some fears while utilizing observation and contemplation. You may or may not remember where something started and that is okay. It is more important to realize and understand the beliefs behind any reaction or obstacle. It is then that you will feel more able to challenge your behaviors by applying new choices in the here and now. New reality-based choices are likely to create change. If you make choices on the basis of a 'should' or a habitual faulty perspective, then the choice might be feeding a need for predictability, a fear-based belief, or an imaginary story. When you create the intention to see the truth within yourself through inner witnessing on a regular basis, you will catch these historical programs as they arise. Ongoing contemplation will be needed. Through conscious purposeful choice and participation, change can come. Continue practicing as often as you can.

What have you discovered from this exercise?

_____
_____
_____
_____
_____
_____
_____
_____
_____
_____
_____
_____
_____
_____
_____
_____
_____
_____
_____
_____
_____
_____

Transitioning Beyond Your Conditioned Blueprint

_____
_____
_____
_____
_____
_____
_____
_____
_____
_____
_____
_____

Witnessing and contemplation are tools that give you greater clarity and discernment in everyday life. Continued practice brings freedom from the enslavement of unconscious behaviors. This can be practiced on the spot in solo or shared situations.

When you bring this practice into shared experiences, it will seem more challenging. However, you are without a doubt already utilizing it some of the time. Contemplation likely happens when you are in a relaxed state or comfortable with your situation and other people. Whenever you seek to understand something, you are likely contemplating.

You can begin to practice observing yourself in shared exchanges to see if you can recognize when your interactions are authentic and when they are habitual. Notice the ease at which your exchanges occur. It is effortless when you are participating from a position of authenticity. However, if you see yourself giving habitual responses, if you compete with others, or if you are trying to be the center of attention, there will likely be some degree of tension or a struggle at the basis of your interaction. In this case, you will not have access to the larger picture, and contemplation most often will not occur naturally. When you catch this happening, apply contemplation. These behaviors can be contemplated either after the fact or in the moment if possible. If you say no to the behavior, you can create a brief internal space for contemplation. You can also say no to the behavior while creating the intention to discover more about the other person.

If your intention is to witness the other person and you are getting distracted by your own thoughts, make a comment or as a question. This can create a pause from your own inner dialog. You might say, "I see; that is interesting; I understand where you are coming from, etc. Or you can ask a question such as, "Can you describe that further? What was that like for you? Why do you think that you chose that?" Your questions create a receptive pause which gives enough space for you to discover something. You are simply giving your full attention to the experience. Contemplate what other people share as well as your own response or reactions. Practice seeing others as they are instead of adding an assumption, analysis, or stories about them. Create a commitment to alternate your present moment, fine-tuned focus between yourself and the other people. Notice the details what is happening in the here and now. Also notice the distractions that are created from your own internal habits, themes, stories, judgments, projections, emotions, and fantasies. Then use contemplation and see what you discover. You can practice periodically throughout the day, on your own or with others. You can decide how far you want to take this.

This practice can be utilized to whatever degree suits your individual needs. For example, you can embrace this approach for the purpose of understanding and transforming reactions, to identify and understand faulty beliefs, to gain a greater understanding of others, or to perceive the larger picture of any situation, and discover new possibilities. It could be that you practice contemplation only in certain situations, or you use it for a means of becoming clearer on a daily basis. If you incorporate it so that it becomes a natural part of your processing, then your struggles with life and your suffering will be greatly diminished. You will find that you are more often present, have regular insights about yourself, other people, your experiences, and you have a greater sense of peace. You may even have moments of feeling complete harmony with all of life. Curiosity and contemplation will open the door to the deepest level of your authentic being and help you to access a level of consciousness, which is your pure self.

The following is an example of how a lifelong practice of presence and contemplation can bring about a realization of pure consciousness within the substance which connects all of life.

Transitioning Beyond Your Conditioned Blueprint

This story is about a woman by the name of Davina. She had been spiritually focused most of her life. During one of her spiritual retreats, she spent many days in a constant state of presence and deep contemplation. Many insights came to her. One afternoon after sitting at length, she decided to take a walk. Upon exiting the door, a turkey vulture with a six-foot wingspan flew just above, within five feet of her head. The sight of it was other-worldly. She continued the walk.

Five minutes later when walking down the road, she became aware of a shame/blame pattern within herself. It was a pattern of taking on false shame through the projected blame of others. She began to inwardly observe, and many truths gracefully unfolded. She could see a whole lineage of this pattern extending back on her mother's side through many generations. She saw it to be merely a history of false belief. As the truth anchored on an experiential level, Davina felt bright, expanded, and alive with her surroundings. Through realizing the origin and falsity of the belief, it dissolved away while understanding and wisdom remained. It was alive as an experiential knowing. She felt light, free, and aware of a union with the depth of creation. This feeling became otherworldly to the point where she had the experience of being vibrantly alive in connection with everything. The trees were no longer just trees, they were pure life force or Divine energy – as was everything else, including herself.

When the retreat ended Davina resumed her regular life. The experience of oneness continued for weeks. During that time, she sometimes felt something else attempting to emerge from the experience of wholeness – like a piece of consciousness looking for a role. It felt like her conditioned personal "I". This conditioned "I" presence would briefly appear and then disappear until the day that Davina had a doctor's appointment.

As she walked into the office building for her appointment, she proceeded down a very long hallway. There was a feeling of bliss and wholeness within her. As she entered the doctor's office, she felt unity with the people there. Then suddenly something shifted. A sense of fear appeared along with the thought, "Maybe I feel so peaceful and at one with everything because I am going to die right now." Panic was taking over, but it was still observable. Davina realized that it was the "I" presence – the ego. The conditioned ego-self had been there in a diminished way, and it was afraid of disappearing. As Davina continued to observe, the fear subsided, but the ego had gained a foothold to some degree once again. A greater, cleaner sense of presence remained, but there was still more work to be done.

Contemplation will help you to clearly perceive ego roles and unhealthy imagination, which are obstacles for most people. It is essential to learn how to recognize the difference between basic truth and fantasy. When considering different choices, look at your feelings and needs in relation to the real details of your overall situation. You must also be able to distinguish the difference between real choice vs. desires and projections that come from a basis of judgment. Desires are made up of pieces of unconscious fantasy. Judgment is full of personalized, projected stories and set ideas. This discernment is essential for making purposeful choices. As you develop discernment, wisdom and insight will regularly rise up from within.

Chapter Two

Uncovering the Fantasy within

-6-

What is fantasy and how can I recognize it?

Fantasy can be made up of imaginary details such as assumptions or judgments involving likes and dislikes, or personalized suggestions that are incorporated into basic perceptions. They often include ideas of what you think should, could be, or should not be taking place. These extra ideas may not be true or possible at the time that they were created or at all – ever. An idea of *should* or *could be,* will inevitably lead to a dependency on what others are doing or not doing, and the creation of inaccurate stories. It will not be purposeful. If you don't know how to recognize the difference between fantasy and basic truth, this can lead to internal drama, distorted projected ideas, judgment, blame, gossip, hostility, fear, competition, self-righteousness, and resistance which will likely bring harm to yourself and others. It can also lead to confusion over available choices. If you habitually struggle with your own thoughts and emotions, then there is a good chance that you have learned patterns of habitual participation with unhealthy imagination. This would include attachment to desired ideas rather than acceptance of present or past experiences, along with an inability to effectively navigate the ongoing facts of present reality.

How does this happen? Many factors can lead people to go off track from the factual details of life. Perhaps they were not taught how to discern between fact and fantasy. Without this discernment, there is no clear process for gracefully navigating one's experiences. A person will try to work things out more so on a mental level rather than through inquiry and direct participation with life. The need to predict will lead to more fantasy as well as specific rules that reinforce the fantasy. When things do not work out, the person will blame outside circumstances rather than recognizing that their imagination misled them. The result will be more stories. The propensity to participate in stories will end up being part of the person's historical foundational blueprint for processing life.

Sometimes people are unknowingly indoctrinated into limiting beliefs from the messages of particular ideologies. These messages may come from culture, race, religion, politics, economic position, gender, generational history, and immediate present-day family conditioning. The limited suggestions inherent in labels will also eclipse possible new discoveries. An ideology or a label has the potential to decide something for someone in a comprehensive manner. This leaves a person's likelihood of receiving what they truly need at the mercy of chance. With this approach, a person is likely to experience significant disappointment and reactive, fantasy-driven thoughts. Historically shared beliefs and practices limit a person's potential to embrace the ever-changing experiences of life.

Fragmented, fantasy-based programming can develop early in life. For example, a caretaker might unreasonably expect a child to consistently know what is expected. This will teach the child to project and/or fantasize in an effort to create predictability. Or it may be that the child is rarely validated, supported, or encouraged, but is criticized instead. In that case the child may develop a fantasy or a hope of being seen, understood, supported, and loved. The fantasy may become more desirable than reality. This would set up a later life potential of choosing and trusting their fantasy in challenging or harmful situations instead of making an appropriate safe choice. A child may also be coddled so that they feel entitled and expect others to take care of them later on. Their greatest tendency would be to imagine someone else figuring things out for them. The person would imagine others tending to their needs instead of having an awareness of how to navigate their own responsibilities and choices. In either case, the child's own authentic needs and unrealized potential will take a secondary position as fantasy scenarios dominate. Hopeful ideas or expectations can turn into recurring fantasies or reactions to imaginary circumstances. The subconscious mind will create what is necessary for a sense of belonging and place of safety. Over time, layers of story can become a habitual response to the circumstances of life. Basic facts and real options may not be clearly recognized, or they may appear too scary for the person to acknowledge, believe, and embrace. Fantasy will subconsciously feel like the safer option when it is the familiar approach for navigating life. When this is the case, fantasy functions as an unrecognized obstacle to one's happiness. It distorts the true meaning of a person's experiences and distracts them from understanding themselves or others. They will not be able to effectively learn or develop trust in themself or life. Unhealthy imagination can play a part in all kinds of situations. To gain freedom from this, a person must be able to identify when it occurs so that they can redirect themselves into the simplicity of a present state of awareness. At that point, they can learn the steps to effectively discover and participate in what is real and new. Below are some examples of situations where individuals mix fantasy in with the real details of their experiences.

A woman by the name of Haley was having a hard time letting go of a past intimate relationship with a man named Peter. She was twenty years old and had little experience with healthy romance. The chemistry had been strong between herself and Peter. She described it as intense. They spent a lot of time together. When they were not together, their thoughts were with one another. Peter was married; she was not. This made it complicated. He never spoke of his wife, so it was as if she did not exist. He made comments about himself and Haley being together forever. Then one day he abruptly ended it. There was no explanation. He simply said that he was not able to see her anymore.

Haley felt abandoned and traumatized. She longed for Peter every day, and he did not make it any easier for her. He kept contacting her as well as asking about her when he encountered anyone that she knew. Of course, she would hear about it, so she attached to the idea that they would be together at some point. This consumed her daily thoughts. She was developing a relationship with a version of him that she created in her imagination. As her participation with it grew from a habit to a compulsion, it distracted her from being present in her daily life as well as being able to perceive any other romantic possibilities. If a possibility did present itself, she would find herself comparing how she had felt with Peter to the man who was standing in front of her. There were no potentials who lived up to what she desired through her comparison.

Transitioning Beyond Your Conditioned Blueprint

The imaginary character of Peter was well integrated into a fantasy version of her present life; however, in reality they only had superficial contact. She needed to know what he was thinking and intending, yet she never thought to ask. This created turmoil for her. He took the lead role with any contact between them, so her needs and curiosities could only be met by chance. Because she was unable to access information through direct inquiry, it was impossible to discern the difference between fantasy and truth. Her imagination took the liberty of filling in the unknowns with fantasy scenarios. She unconsciously feared the truth and took comfort in what she had created in her imagination. She was able to fool herself into still feeling loved by Peter some of the time; however, a constant underlying turmoil reminded her that the circumstances did not validate her fantasy. Finally, just when it all became too much for her to bear, he found another lover and stopped contacting her. This forced her to look at what had happened, take responsibility, and apply the newfound wisdom to her life.

This next example takes place with a grown woman and her father named Elliot. Sally's elderly alcoholic father was in her care. She has repeatedly confronted him about secretly getting rides to the liquor store, getting intoxicated, passing out, wetting his pants, hiding alcohol, and then lying about all of it. It had happened hundreds of times. However, each time Sally had a conversation to address the problem with her father, she imagined that her logical firm approach would make him stop drinking. Elliot seemed remorseful and told her that none of it would happen ever again. She suspected that when he made those claims, he was only appeasing her in an effort to make the conflict go away. However, she still became hopeful and was then disappointed when the drinking happened again. The cycle of pretend continued on both sides.

The truth was clear in this situation. Sally's father had an alcohol addiction. He could not comprehend any reason that was adequate enough for him to stop drinking. Because there were no real consequences for his behavior, Elliot was unmotivated to change and did not take his daughters complaints seriously. Sally was attached to the fantasy of what she hoped would happen. Because the fantasy only provided her with an idea for escaping the situation, she always ended up back in it instead of taking purposeful steps for change. She was not able to accept the truth of what she saw to be happening; therefore, she could not access or consider new options. This kept both people in a cycle of suffering.

Eventually, Elliot's health became compromised from the alcohol abuse which landed him in a nursing home.

The next example is about a grown woman named Cynthia and her elderly mother, Mary. Mary lived with Cynthia – she was in her care. The mother was a hoarder for most of her life. As a result of numerous difficult relationships with men, she gave up on intimacy. Her relationships were instead with physical things. On trash day Mary scoured the neighborhood for desirable items from trash cans along the street. She experienced a temporary fulfillment every time she acquired what felt like a treasure. Cynthia never knew what she would find when she came home from work. It could have been a dozen empty jars or beer bottles from someone's recycling barrel. One day it was an old rusty wheelbarrow that was used to carry a birdcage, a broken chair, and an old cat-litter box.

Mary could not seem to understand why her daughter disapproved of her hoarding, so she kept doing it. Her compulsion to find and collect things felt much more desirable than paying attention to the reasons why it was not appropriate. In comparison to the consequence of her daughter having daily turmoil over it, accumulating clutter felt significantly more rewarding than any choices for change. Mary's compulsive behavior negatively affected some of her relationships, the harmony of the home, and distracted her from other more purposeful possibilities in her life. The temporary fulfillment and hits of dopamine enabled her to maintain the fantasy that she was doing something purposeful by rescuing discarded items from the trash. She could pretend that it was not a problem.

Meanwhile, Cynthia imagined that her mother could give up the behavior, and it would suddenly stop. However, there was not a chance of that happening. Her eighty-five-year-old mother had no ability to stop imaging that her behavior was okay. She had lived in unconscious denial for many years. She did not know how to be consciously present and contemplate. After several years of this, Cynthia suffered enough to look within and realize that she had tormented herself by holding onto the idea that her mother would suddenly stop picking trash. It was just a fantasy. She was ready to contemplate the options of either getting a caretaker for her mother or sending her to live with a stay-at-home sibling who could keep an eye on her.

Transitioning Beyond Your Conditioned Blueprint

    This example takes place with a man who was abused by his wife and was very unfulfilled in his marriage. As a means of escaping from it, he developed a fantasy relationship with a famous actress. He began to follow this woman on the internet to the point where it became a daily obsession. It started out as a curiosity, a distraction, and became a fantasy which was fueled by an innocent need to create an escape through the imagination. His imagination kept going with no means of testing the fantasy against reality. When something like this goes on at length, a person can lose sense of what is rational. Eventually this person's fantasy relationship with the actress felt so real that he took a trip to California to find her. Because he had been tracking her on the internet, he was able to locate and go to the area where she was filming. He walked around for a couple of days and did in fact run into her. He found himself face to face with her in a bookstore. They merely exchanged hellos and nothing more. What he experienced then was an appropriate interaction for the actual reality. This brought him crashing down into the truth of his own situation. He realized the fantasy. When a person puts their ideas to the test in the context of reality, life will show them what can or cannot be. However, ideally this must be done with each step in every experience through contemplation as thoughts and details unfold.

    In the next example, two people struggled and judged each other based on their own fantasy of the other person's motives. Cheryl and Eddie were in relationship. Eddie never complimented Cheryl which upset her. She communicated this to him, but he did not feel her complaint to be valid. He wanted her to accept him as he was. At the same time, he felt that she should know how he felt without him having to say anything. When she complained, he perceived it as criticism and neediness. In response, he was resistant toward changing his behavior. Eddie believed Cheryl was picking on him and did not understand why she needed to be complimented. He was not aware that he did not understand. Instead, he imagined her to have unkind motives behind her request.

    This is where questions and contemplation could have brought more clarity. In response to Eddie's refusal, Cheryl thought that he was purposely trying to make her angry and hurt her feelings. She felt that if he loved her, he would compliment her. Because he didn't understand her or even try to, she imagined that he was trying to punish her for wanting compliments and that he did not love her. *Her imagination was attempting to fill in the pieces that did not make sense.* On both sides, there was a need for each person to understand the other through further questioning, sharing, good listening, contemplation, and acceptance. As you can now see, the need for understanding existed but went unrealized. Cheryl and Eddie both needed to be understood, but that need was not comprehended.

This example makes apparent just how dangerous and destructive multi-layered fantasy can be. In this situation two brothers have a disagreement. The youngest brother Fred tends to look for validation from his older brother. Because he lacks confidence, no amount of recognition will ever be enough for Fred. This also makes him competitive. Joe and his wife were hoping to conceive a child; however, a year had gone by, and they were still waiting for it to happen. In the meantime, Fred announced that his girlfriend had become pregnant. Joe was happy for him and acknowledged it by congratulating Fred and his girlfriend. Fred criticized Joe's response as inadequate. He projected the idea that Joe was envious and judgmental of him because he was not married to the woman who was carrying his child. He created an imaginary story and got angry over what he, himself was creating in his own head.

Fred told the imaginary story to his family. He let it be known that he felt victimized by his brother. However, his brother had nothing to do with the imaginary scenario that Fred created. Joe was confused by the accusations. He sought to resolve it, by once again, sharing his real feelings and intentions with his brother. He had hoped that resolution would come through understanding. Fred was afraid to listen to his brother's truth for fear of being wrong. He was not capable of hearing what was being shared. Instead, he held tightly onto the fantasy while believing that he had been wronged. He did not know how to be responsible for or process his mistakes. Fred had misread and misrepresented Joe's intentions due to his own insecurities and inability to be present and process life in a direct manner.

Joe made multiple requests to talk and resolve this, but Fred got angry while further misrepresenting Joe through gossip with family members and others. He made up stories and blamed Joe for many things that never took place. As lies multiplied, he became more afraid of being held accountable to the truth. In order to maintain the fantasy that he had created, he separated himself from Joe and demanded that family members do the same. He did not want to have his

Transitioning Beyond Your Conditioned Blueprint

stories tested against reality. As long as he could keep his fantasy contained, he could continue with it. He pulled others into the drama with the threat to abandon them if they disagreed with him. This dynamic became the dominant focus within the family. Finally, the situation became so toxic that any bonds or trust that had existed between family members were destroyed through participation in the fantasy, confusion, and turmoil.

In this case, the solution would have been to directly acknowledge the overall facts of the situation and participate through curiosity to discover and understand the individual beliefs while discerning fantasy from truth. When people sincerely and honestly share with one another, reality often reveals itself. With honest inquiry and contemplation, what we know and do not know becomes more apparent.

Stereotypes also generate fantasy-based thinking and limiting beliefs. For instance, people sometimes believe that cultural expectations about gender are rules to be followed. This might include - men do not clean the house; men must only show strength; men are the head of the household; it's natural for men to sleep around; a woman will get hurt if she uses power tools or works on a roof; a woman who has multiple sexual partners is immoral; childcare is the sole responsibility of a woman. You get the idea.

The following exercise will help you to distinguish the difference between fantasy and basic facts. You will need to identify a situation where you feel some disappointment, resistance, or judgment toward a person or situation. The struggle can be large or small. It could be anything from a friend not returning a phone call, to losing a job promotion at work. Write down the details of the situation and the feelings that it produced. Then write down the reasons why you feel that way.

What are the beliefs behind your feelings?

_____
_____
_____
_____
_____
_____

Now, take a few minutes and look for the facts of the situation – the circumstances that you know to be true. This includes the details of the experience that are actual, provable facts. This means that you had a direct experience of these facts without making assumptions or adding stories. These facts may be pretty basic once you eliminate the details that you imagined.

Transitioning Beyond Your Conditioned Blueprint

Write down your discoveries.

_____
_____
_____
_____

Now identify any emotional charge that is connected to any part of the memory. Notice if you are *adding* any ideas of should, could have, or if only to the situation. Notice any hope, blame, or resentment. Do not allow yourself to jump into any of these feelings; they are based on fantasies. If you are already doing this, bring your focus within, take a step back, and witness yourself. This means that you are not immersing yourself as an actor in the drama. Instead, you witness yourself attempting to do it. When you refrain from being a full participant in the imaginary pieces of a situation, you will be creating an internal boundary.

Write down any imagined details. Remember, these are pieces of projected stories which are often formulated from judgment, resistance, blame, desires, etc. These details were not directly experienced.

_____
_____
_____
_____
_____
_____
_____
_____
_____
_____
_____
_____
_____
_____
_____
_____
_____
_____
_____

Transitioning Beyond Your Conditioned Blueprint

_____
_____
_____
_____
_____
_____
_____
_____

Through your inner inquiry you will likely become aware of some details that you have fabricated about yourself, other people, or situations. Once these are identified, you can ask yourself some of the following questions. Do I feel fear or resistance toward taking responsibility for the truth? Why do I choose to engage with self-created fantasy versions of other people, rather than participating directly with real people? Why do I believe that it is okay to define a person's entire identity on the basis of a personal judgment or something that I do not like about them? Why do I create fantasy versions of myself, along with the expectation that other people should participate with the fantasies by pretending that they are real? Can I identify any long term or short-term value in this behavior? How is this behavior bringing harm to myself and others? In what ways am I limiting my own option to live a fuller and more purposeful life?

Write down your discoveries.

_____
_____
_____
_____
_____
_____
_____
_____
_____
_____
_____
_____

Some of the scenarios that you imagine may end up happening. However, if you worry about a possible outcome, you will likely create emotional distress and drain your own energy. It's one thing to be aware of possibilities; it's another thing to act like ideas are real before anything has happened. They may or may not come about. Instead, it is best to participate in each experience as it unfolds. Trust that you are capable of perceiving and acting on the best possible options in each situation as the need arises. You will be more focused, clearer minded, much stronger, and more capable when you are present instead of worried.

It is also possible that your intuition is showing you something true. When an intuitive insight arises, it will not feel personal even if it pertains to you. It will not carry an emotional charge. This means that it did not come from your ego; it came from a much deeper more authentic level of consciousness. A deep sense of knowing often comes with an insight. If an emotional reaction is intimately intertwined with your thought, then it probably came from your imagination. If you do experience what seems like a truly intuitive insight, do not create a story around it. Instead, pay attention, use discernment, but do not go into reaction. If you are accustomed to having insights, pay special attention when they occur. Otherwise, make your choices for each situation based on the reality that you see before you. When you are present, it becomes easy to discern fantasy from intuition. Fantasy most often has an emotional charge in it, whereas intuition has a stillness and sometimes a sense of deep knowing. Fantasy has an element of personalization, whereas intuition does not.

Now, let's continue to practice discerning truth from fantasy. Once again bring your focus inward to observe and contemplate a situation that involves disappointment, resistance, or judgment. Your goal is to practice identifying the individual pieces of fact and fantasy as they emerge in your awareness. When a truth appears say to yourself, "That is true." When a fantasy appears say to yourself, "That is an imaginary detail or that is a story. I do not know that to be true. I have not had any direct experience of that being true."

Look to see if you are taking on an imaginary role or creating an embellishment. Remember, to pretend is to participate with something that has not been confirmed through direct experience. If you are pretending, is it fueled and influenced by unconscious fear, desire, a temporary fulfillment through distraction, or a faulty belief? If you notice this happening, then acknowledge it. Take some time to acknowledge the truth of what you are perceiving. Contemplate it, and then state what you see out loud so that you experience it and hear it. In this way you will be processing the truth of what you perceive on multiple levels. You will only be stating real facts that have been directly experienced.

Now make the following statement to yourself, "I am capable of distinguishing truth from fantasy more and more each day. I now make the decision to consciously choose from a basis of truth to the best of my ability in each situation." Throughout this exercise you have been embracing a process of creating internal space through witnessing and curiosity, discerning the difference between facts and imagination as well as creating a new starting point, redirecting your perceptions, and learning how to meet yourself and life in the moment. The questioning and act of conscious acknowledgement will also help you to create more space in your witnessing practice. It will also bring unconscious compulsive patterns of thought and belief into a conscious state, so that you can gain understanding and make new choices.

When you feel that you have reached enough confidence to discern the difference between fantasy and truth, then you can go a step further to identify possible solutions for your struggle. Perhaps you will have to let go of a faulty idea that maintained your attachment to a particular fantasy. You may need to make further discoveries through inner questioning or make inquires of others. You will also have to let go of any expectations about a timeframe for results from this new approach. Sometimes when the fantasy is removed a broad understanding and new options become obvious. At other times, you will need to be patient and allow the answers and understanding to unfold. What have you discovered through your inquiry so far?

Write down your discoveries.

Transitioning Beyond Your Conditioned Blueprint

Now, based on the truth of your discoveries, write down your chosen first step toward the exploration and creation of something new.

_____
_____
_____
_____
_____
_____

At this point you are likely to have a clearer understanding of how mental/emotional fantasy is created and how it can complicate your life. To recap, you may misinterpret a situation. As a result of the misinterpretation, you will desire something else and get stuck in a judgment or a false belief that is fueled by a lack of understanding. Next, you may feel resistance to discovering something new. When this occurs, pieces of information have been taken out of context and imaginary details have been added which creates a false interpretation of the situation. At that point, you have lost the ability to witness, seek more information, apply discernment, and negotiate truth; you are in a compulsive interaction with the self. For an understanding of the larger picture and discernment of truth vs. fantasy, you need the ability to step back and witness. If the fantasy goes on at length, it may well evolve into a full-blown drama. The reactions that emerge from the drama will take on a compulsive nature. When this occurs, there will be no room for discovery unless a discovery process is consciously implemented. Without new discoveries, all of the participants may suffer. This is a cyclical process; it will continue until discernment is applied through witnessing and contemplation.

-7-

Dependence on fantasy for a sense of comfort and safety

In this situation, the person has little to no experience of being supported in their individuality and has not been taught a process for building skills or reaching goals. As a result, they sometimes identify with imaginary roles of success instead of stepping out to participate, learn, and grow. A sense of personal value may be so foreign that it can only exist for the person through a relationship with

Transitioning Beyond Your Conditioned Blueprint

imagined versions of themself. A person will often refer to these fantasy versions through statements such as, "I could have been or I'm going to be a successful person." Sometimes they go as far as to claim that they have achieved something when they have not. However, they will make no sustained effort to attain any such position. When the person feels built up or strengthened from simply thinking about the role, it may fulfill an unsatisfied need for a short period of time. The person may have created the fantasy role to compensate for a particular area of their life that remained unfulfilled. If a need arose for unbridled joy, the person may imagine that they could have been a singer or dancer. If a person has no money due to unforeseen circumstances, self-sabotage, or a gambling addiction, they may find momentary comfort through a fantasy of being rescued or suddenly having a big win and becoming wealthy. If they consistently feel the need to defend themself or they feel that a sense of an injustice has occurred, they may connect with the idea that they could have been an attorney or a detective. When there is an unmet need to be heard or understood, the person may focus on the idea of being a writer or professor.

The fantasy self becomes a source of support for them. They may be getting enough out of the fantasy on some level so that a need to act upon it is never realized. It might also be that they do not want to act upon it because it unconsciously provides a sense of safety and comfort. In that case, the idea of it would be held in a safe place - untouched by the individual's real life. The predictability of connecting with it would soften the blow of not knowing how to resolve suffering or take steps to discover their full potential. All of this behavior is carried out unconsciously.

The person may revert to this fantasy version of the self for nurturing when they feel a void or vulnerability; however, it will have a dual effect. They may momentarily feel good, but at the same time, it will feel like a loss of something even though they never had it and don't truly know if it would be possible in reality. None of this can be known if the person has not stepped out of their comfort zone to challenge themself.

Can you identify any unconscious dependency on a fantasy role? Write down the details.

_____
_____

Can you identify what you are getting out of it as well as how it keeps you stuck? To what degree are you attached to the story? Can you identify any

Transitioning Beyond Your Conditioned Blueprint

personal harm from your participation with it? Are you resistant or afraid to let go of your fantasy? If so, contemplate these things, and see what you discover.

Write down your discoveries.

_____

Do you recognize any steps that you can take toward changing the ways that you participate so that you can test the fantasy to determine whether it can be real or not? Also, would you truly want to make it a real part of your life?

Write down your discoveries.

_____

-8-

How does fantasy influence procrastination?

Fantasy encourages and reinforces pretend, avoidance, and procrastination. When you are procrastinating, the ego is compulsively deciding things for you. Perhaps you tell yourself things such as, "That is going to be too difficult; I don't think that I can get enough motivation for that; I'm not sure that I am capable of doing that today; I think that it could take too much time." With all of these suggestions, the conditioned mind is deciding things without having had a direct experience of the task or objective. It can be very convincing. However, it is important to challenge what it is telling you.

When procrastination occurs, witness your thoughts, and challenge your conditioned mind by allowing yourself to access some understanding through contemplation. Then make a choice to participate directly. Start out by giving yourself fifteen minutes to participate in a direct experience with the task. This will often reveal to you something quite different from what the mind was suggesting. It may be useful to engage with the task for another fifteen minutes so that you can make further discoveries. At that point, you will be equipped to make a conscious choice to continue or not. Each time you find yourself procrastinating apply this new approach, and you will soon reprogram the pattern.

-9-

Two examples of fantasy scenarios with steps for transforming them

The first example involves a woman who created an imaginary scenario in a work situation. This woman believed that her boss would fire her if she did not perform perfectly, according to *her idea of* what he expected from her.

1. If you can relate to this example, bring your focus inward to witness your struggle. Then through curiosity, notice your beliefs. Determine if they are assumed or fact based. The assumptions are based in imaginary ideas – not facts. They did not come from direct experience. Take a moment to acknowledge this.
2. Take responsibility for discerning the difference between truth and fantasy. Remember, if you have not had a direct experience that confirms your ideas, then you must participate to discover the facts of reality or allow your experiences to unfold further while consciously participating with direct, honest, purposeful choices and inquiry.
3. Ask yourself some of the following questions. Are these thought processes useful for me? What am I getting out of this? Am I putting undo

pressure onto myself and others with my fears or presumptions? In what way am I being harmed by my own thoughts? What might I be missing, and what is needed to access more understanding? Am I trying to make life predictable by trying to control it through projections?

4. As you ask these questions, you may realize that your imagination has been bullying you. With this recognition, ask yourself, "Would I stand for this if it was coming from another person?" It is likely that you would not. Once you see the truth of what is happening, it is much easier to create boundaries with your imagination and make new choices for discovery and change.
5. Next you can make some new alternate conscious choices with the way that you engage with yourself as well as with others.
6. Accept that your capacity to know is determined by direct participation and inquiry.
7. *You cannot know what has not yet occurred. Likewise, you cannot expect that you should or could have known something that you are only just now discovering.*

Know that a process to change any behavior will take place over a span of time. Through continued interruption of untruths and redirection of purposeful intentions, choices, and actions, you will make ongoing discoveries.

This next example is about a mother who believes that her children will be damaged if she does not give perfect guidance for every challenge and struggle that they face. Because this woman never sees her guidance as being good enough, she perceives herself as a failed mother.

If you can relate to any part of this, the following considerations may be helpful.

1. Start by questioning your beliefs. You can use the following sample questions or some of your own. Do these beliefs have any real value to me? Who created the beliefs? Is it useful to imagine myself as a failure as well as imagining that others see me as a failure? Am I willing to accept my own value as an individual human being? Am I willing to accept the value of my parenting skills? Do I accept responsibility for changing my behavior by challenging my perspectives and choosing differently?

2. Next, look at the many people who have influenced your children besides yourself. Your children likely interact with an extended family, your friends, their friends, teachers, and childcare workers as well as other people out in society. They watch TV, and if they are old enough, they spend time with technology. Realistically, your influence can only go so far. Each child enters the world as a unique individual with their own behavior and capabilities. Genetic programming plays a large part in your child's identity too. You likely have far less influence than you would like to believe.
3. Accept the degree of influence that you have. Know that your child is a unique individual. The child cannot be an exact copy of you, your values, perspectives, interests, beliefs, or personal experience.
4. Always expand your view out into the larger picture. Your keys for doing this are curiosity, witnessing, contemplation, questions, and applying new choices with ongoing participation.

As you look and inquire into the larger picture of any situation, you will gain understanding about yourself, other people, and your long-standing reactions. Those reactions can become doorways through which you can enter your subconscious, facilitate change, and transition yourself into a greater experience of presence. They provide a bridge for accessing wisdom and then transition you into a state of greater self-awareness. They give you access to your subconscious and beyond. The subconscious is where all deprogramming and reprogramming takes place. You can best utilize the reactions when they are active, not after the fact. That activated feeling is your bridge to the subconscious. If you try to mentally process through a memory, most of the time, you will only be processing on a surface level which is ineffective. Remember, conscious participation brings about gradual change through many steps. For ongoing change, your commitment to the process must be in place. Remember, you must pause within yourself and witness. This creates space and disengages you from the act of personalization.

Space broadens the doorway to make room for discovery. Without having the space to witness and contemplate, the possibility of recognizing healthy, purposeful, effective choices will be less likely or may only happen by chance. Next, I will provide you with more information about space.

Chapter Three

Understanding Internal Space

-10-

How can I better understand, create, and make effective use of internal space?

A space within your experience is the pause or emptiness between your feelings, ideas, and the facts of the situation. Allowing this space to exist is necessary for rational thinking and choice making. If you don't have enough of this space, you will feel trapped by your own thoughts and emotions. You will also experience some degree of confusion or overwhelm. It is not possible to effectively navigate your inner reality without it. The space is a stillness or pause that naturally supports deep experience and discovery. It is a non-doing, non-grasping state. As you participate with inner space, you will access the substance and wisdom of your everyday experiences more easily. Also, whenever a reaction or compulsion exists, more space is needed to process, understand, and transition it. When you surrender to become the space or pause, the innate stillness supports access to your authentic, intuitive self. In the moment processing naturally occurs. Everyone experiences this space on a regular basis; however, many people are not consciously aware of it and don't know how to access it by choice.

You may recognize the space within you when you are very present and listening to music or to someone else talking. There is pause that invites what is being shared. You may also notice it when you are present in a relaxed state; there is no forward agenda dominating you. It can be recognized when you have surrendered into the complete presence of an experience in nature as you watch the clouds or take in the beauty of a landscape. It is the act of surrendering into the space that facilitates a sense of openness, aliveness, and inner freedom. When space is a balanced part of your everyday experience, your attention will not be possessed by an individual thought or theme. There is a harmonious interplay between the thoughts, emotions, and the deeper experiential level of being. There is a quality of grace within your experience. It is without a dualistic or black and white process. Everything has a natural relationship. Both trust and surrender are present as you transition from one detail to the next. It will feel satisfying and safe to interact with another person when they are in this mode of functioning. It is naturally fulfilling. Over time, as you learn to naturally embrace space, you will feel comfortable interacting in most any type of situation.

Some examples of situations that may activate inner space are kayaking, walking in nature, creating art, playing a musical instrument, and creative writing. As you become one with the experience, you settle into a quality of being that is effortless. It is often referred to as "being in the zone." The space comes with the act of surrender and complete attention. You become the experience. This can also be recognized when someone is creatively trouble shooting from a place of confidence instead of fear. Again, there is an open space that allows for a stream of creative/intuitive experience to gracefully unfold without you trying to make it happen.

Additionally, when you taste something for the first time there is an open receptivity within you that is space. The pause is happening when you feel curious about the new flavor. However, the opposite would be true if you were to create a prejudgment of the food. With prejudgment, there would be no space for discovery. There would be a closed off feeling which would be resistance. This is the opposite of a surrendered, present state of consciousness.

Worry is something else that will close off the space within you. When the mind appears to be stuck in worry, it is a reaction to fear. The fear will attach to specific themes in a cyclical manner. This is because the subconscious is attempting to access a solution or predictable outcome through pieces of fragmented or imagined experiences that have not yet happened. This will not create space. It will create the opposite – the feeling of being trapped and needing to escape. With the occurrence of worry, space can be created by consciously shifting your focus into the present moment while discerning the difference between real details and projected ideas. Choose to put your focus only on the real details and available choices. When there are no purposeful, available choices to make, then you must let the situation further unfold, or if possible, inquire to access more information. If you are having trouble accessing space or shifting your focus, then take a brisk walk, go for a run, do something creative, sing a song, or go for a bike ride. Any of these activities have the potential to ground you and give you some internal space from the problem. Physical activity, such as running, fools the primal self into believing that it is escaping. At that point, you can utilize the space that you created for witnessing, contemplation, making discoveries, or you can simply be in a broader, freer internal experience.

Another experience of limited space occurs when people engage in a heated disagreement. They will be fixated on what they think they know. The thought processes and communications will often take place in a closed-down, cyclical manner. When an argument is taking place, it is possible to create a pause by asking a question or stating something like, "Let me think about that." Or perhaps you say, "I realize that I do not completely understand. Can you tell me in another way or share your beliefs behind the point that you are trying to make?" Another response might be, "I can see that you are feeling that way, or yes, I understand that you do perceive that to be the right way." By choosing to engage in a non-confrontational manner or to ask a question, you are inviting some space and activating a state of curiosity. When people are arguing, they often make unconscious statements about the need to understand, while being unable to realize how to do it. You may recall hearing comments such as, "Can you just be open, or can you consider what I am saying?" In this case, make it a point to pause and listen. Then acknowledge the person and what they are saying to you. Some helpful statements are, "I want to understand; I'm listening, or I do understand. Can you please tell me more?" Also, an open-ended question will initiate a pause – an opening up of a space. It can be beneficial when you repeat what you hear back to the person who spoke it. In this way they will know that you are listening.

When the practice of unattached openness is learned through regular participation with daily witnessing or meditation, then the space becomes recognizable and spontaneously accessible. It then becomes a choice – a simple shift of focus. You can learn to access it in your daily life thru ongoing practice. This pause or place of stillness is also a doorway to presence, your subconscious, and your all-knowing Divine self. This is the place from which true knowing emerges.

Additional ways that you can create presence and space are through activities that bring you to an experiential level. Some of these may include running, Tai Chi, yoga, playful interaction with a child, free-flowing humor, and humming. They all have the potential to bring about inner space when you become immersed within the experience. If you participate primarily through a dominant mind, then little space or free flowing experience will take place. When you make any conscious choice and remain curious, you are transitioning yourself into the space of the moment. Witnessing is a natural part of *in the moment* experience. When you do this, life is more interesting and fulfilling even when you are participating in the commonplace activities of everyday life. Examples of such activities may include cleaning your refrigerator, changing diapers, raking leaves, washing dishes, doing paperwork, vacuuming, paying bills, etc. If you wholeheartedly commit yourself to a state of presence with an experience, a spaciousness will naturally be there.

When your inner experience becomes cleaner, you can utilize the space or stillness to intentionally contemplate any struggles in an unattached manner while using curiosity to access a broader understanding and a deep knowing. When you sit with an experience and watch it, you will see and realize things that were not obvious to you beforehand. You must approach it as if you were tasting a new variety of food. You are present, open, and receptive while being unattached to anything specific.

Can you identify any habitual personal approach or situation that needs more internal space? Describe it.

_____
_____
_____
_____

Transitioning Beyond Your Conditioned Blueprint

_____
_____
_____
_____
_____
_____
_____
_____
_____
_____
_____
_____
_____
_____
_____
_____
_____
_____
_____
_____
_____
_____
_____
_____
_____
_____
_____

Now, can you identify some possibilities for making space? Write down your discoveries. Then set your intentions to practice this whenever possible.

_____
_____
_____
_____
_____
_____

Once you learn how to create inner space and witness yourself on a regular basis, you will quickly realize the degree to which many behaviors and thought patterns have been filling up your inner space. Some of these may include ongoing inner chatter, cyclical scenarios of conflict, unhealthy imagination, struggles with fragmented perspectives, and judgment-filled thinking. When your inner space is possessed by compulsive behavior, there will be no room to just be, contemplate, or access the deeper wisdom of your life. This can lead to many destructive behaviors. When you personalize, judge, or have a rigid agenda, you close the birthing process of the next moment. This is when a stream of fantasy is likely to be interjected into your experience from the ego.

For example, the space will surely close if you imagine that another person will reject you because that individual is more attractive, smarter, more social, from another race or economic status, worldlier, etc. These become fixed ideas that create blanket perceptions as well as a barrier toward presence, space, authentic participation, and discovery.

In another variation, a conditioned reaction could lead to an instant, limited, inauthentic analysis of someone else. You have probably heard some version of the following statements: "Oh, that person looks like my nasty old boss or my mean uncle. I will never trust him or her." Or another example could be, "Man, look at that hot body! I would love to be married to someone like that." The mind can quickly conjure up a disapproving or appealing fantasy that can cut off the mode of discovery. When this occurs, the opportunity to experience someone as a whole person is lost.

As you now contemplate, do you recognize any space-limiting behaviors within yourself? Do you recognize any specific situations where those patterns block the possibility of discovery or create limitation or suffering?

Write down your understanding of them along with ideas for creating space.

_____
_____
_____
_____
_____
_____
_____
_____
_____
_____
_____
_____
_____
_____

Now, when you see yourself overtaken by judgments, desires, and unhealthy behaviors, you can consciously choose to bring your focus inward, become curious, create space, identify, and contemplate the beliefs that underlie your behavior patterns, and seek to gain understanding through inward questioning. An inner space naturally opens up when you do this. The questions and new understanding can lead to deep realizations, discoveries, new possibilities, and eventually free you from harmful imagination and habitual behaviors. More details about inner and outer space will be discussed later in the book. For now, we will look at some other behaviors that reinforce an unconscious state.

Chapter Four

Compulsions and Engaging Your Inner Warrior

-11-

What is a compulsion and what can I do about it?

Compulsions are the driving force at the root of destructive behavior and addiction. Addictive behavior can take place with the overuse of food, chemical substances, or participation with fantasy through drama, video games, overuse of technology, porn, gambling, shopping, excessive accumulation of possessions, etc. If your compulsion involves an addiction to alcohol or a chemical substance, you may need to first go through a detox program and then address the compulsive behaviors through self-awareness.

The uncontrolled impulses which come from compulsions can also be seen with a broad range of behaviors and routine emotional reactions such as: the need to be right, a feeling of entitlement, an attachment to dominating and processing the experiences of others, over-identification as a victim, the use of anger used to control others, the use of judgment to control others, or the use of blame to avoid personal responsibility, or a resistance to learning from your mistakes. Sometimes the emotional-reactive compulsion exists as the original addiction, and then other more recognizable ones, such as alcohol or drug use, gambling, hoarding, overeating, or porn get added onto the original compulsive-emotional reactive pattern. For example, a compulsive-emotional reaction could get created when people feel powerless against ongoing acts of wrong made toward them. They may routinely get caught up in a compulsive-emotional reaction that is fueled by a faulty belief about being powerless. They may not know how to look within to explore options beyond the belief, choose differently, or perhaps create external boundaries with their circumstances or internal boundaries within their own mind. Instead, they may complain about being wronged and habitually identify with a drama state while gaining a momentary false sense of power through venting with others. Because the drama does not resolve the reactive issue, they resort to drinking alcohol or using substances to numb themself in response to the powerless state. Hence you have a compulsive-addictive behavior layered on top of a pattern of a compulsive-emotional reaction.

In another scenario, maybe someone is routinely criticized, so that person develops a fear of being seen as faulty and being rejected. Hence, they approach life from the position of believing that others will see them as wrong. They compulsively react with false shame.

Perhaps someone else routinely feels dismissed and unheard. They become angry, feel empowered by the anger, and identify with it as a place of safety. That becomes their automatic go-to reaction when conflict arises. However, the anger only provides momentary false safety through a temporary sense of dominance. Because the conflict is not resolved, the anger is repeated in a cyclical manner that brings endless turmoil for the one creating it. When this becomes unbearable, it is likely that a compulsive-addictive behavior will be added such as overeating, gambling, etc.

Once the compulsive-emotional reaction is established, the essence of the theme or belief that created it will be triggered in certain circumstances. The more it is activated, the more the mind will distort reality to fit the beliefs within the reaction or the theme. Examples may be, "I will always be blamed for something; they will not hear me; people think that I am stupid; I will be harmed in the presence of others; I always have to defend myself; others will try to take away my value; people will always judge me." Once the belief is activated, the person will personalize and distort their perceptions of a situation to fit the belief or theme.

Sometimes the compulsive-addictive behaviors do develop without having a compulsive-emotional reaction at the foundation. They exist purely as a physical chemical addiction. In that case, it is likely that compulsive-emotional reactions will be birthed from the fragmented state of the physical-chemical addiction. From the examples given, you can see that faulty beliefs lay a foundation of compulsive-emotional reactions that may then lead to a compulsive-addictive behavior. This is the case a majority of the time. These faulty beliefs may come about from unprocessed trauma, inadequate skills for processing life, an inability to access the self in the present moment, to witness, or to make discoveries through curiosity-based inquiry or contemplation.

Most often compulsive-addictive behaviors gradually develop. A compulsive-addictive behavior sometimes starts out as a simple choice connected to a desire for pleasure or for relief from suffering. Sometimes the choice is made from an unconscious or conscious need to escape the discomfort of not being in control of something, an inability to meet an emotional need, to find relief from an unprocessed trauma, escape from ongoing stress, or to relieve a fear or feel temporarily fulfilled, etc. The subconscious mind identifies with the satisfactory result. When the choice is repeated, it may turn into a tendency and progress further. For example, some individuals may be inclined to go shopping or have a drink when they feel stress. At first, the action is conscious and controllable. A sense of cause and effect will be clearly accessible when making the choice. However, if the choice becomes frequent, the space around it shrinks as the desire and behavior increases. At that juncture a habit is created. Logic begins to lose its ground. An attachment to the desired outcome gathers strength. It is harder to access reason, though reason is still there in a limited way. If the frequency of the habit continues to increase, the habit is likely to turn into a compulsion. At that point, it becomes an unconscious choice with a desire and action that nearly or completely has full control of you. The choice becomes automatic rather than conscious. Your perception of consequences may not be there at all, or they may seem like a faint shadow in the background of your awareness. The perception of consequences may at best seem like a very faint whisper of a warning. It is so small that it is likely to be ignored. As you recall various compulsive experiences, do you remember asking yourself questions like, "How did that happen? What was I thinking? Or why did I do that?" Know that this happens because any internal space and the experience of presence has been lost. A compulsion does not leave room for a person to process or contemplate before the action is taken.

When a person makes an unconscious compulsive choice, which results in unpleasant consequences, it will lead to confusion. The confusion may then lead to self-doubt, and feelings of powerlessness, sadness, shame, anger, self-judgment, fear, guilt, and lead to acts of secrecy or blame. When people do not rationally understand something, they will not feel safe and will want to hide, pretend, or escape the experience through avoidance, distortion of facts, or blame. Can you identify with any of this as you contemplate your own experiences?

If so, write down the details.

_____
_____
_____
_____
_____
_____
_____
_____
_____
_____
_____
_____
_____
_____
_____
_____
_____
_____
_____
_____
_____
_____
_____
_____
_____
_____

-12-

Transitioning compulsions back into conscious choices

Now that you understand how a compulsion gets created and how it works, you can begin to turn the compulsions back into conscious choices. If your compulsion involves an addiction to alcohol or a chemical substance, you may need to go through a detox program first; then you can address the compulsive actions and emotional reactions through self-awareness practices.

To begin, it is very important to develop a practice of witnessing and to contemplate your faulty beliefs, reactions, resistance, etc. Every compulsion is made up of some of these behavioral components. Therefore, when you shift any of these into a position of truth, you are altering the substance of the compulsion. It is just as important to develop an ability to discern between unhealthy fantasy-based thinking and basic facts. When something is unknown, the mind will sometimes imagine and project ideas rather than exploring further to discover what is real. The compulsions are filled with partially processed experiences, faulty beliefs, and serve as an escape from direct, honest participation and discovery. Your most predominant compulsions will be very charged and often overpowering. They will strike like a lightning bolt, and you won't see them coming. In the beginning you will only be able to contemplate your experience of them after the fact. This is still beneficial. This practice will begin to prime your conscious mind to recognize the compulsions. This is your first step for introducing space around them. Take some time to practice this. It will likely take weeks for this part to become automatic. For the compulsions to be transitioned back into a position of a simple choice, they need a lot of space reestablished with them. There will be more steps presented for this transitioning process as we proceed. However, it is important to simultaneously practice shifting the compulsive-emotional reactions.

Since many of the compulsive-emotional reactions are less charged than the drive behind the more pronounced compulsive-addictive behaviors, it can be a bit easier to catch them in the moment rather than after the fact. When a compulsion is addressed in one area, the effect is holistic to some degree. The most common compulsive-emotional reactions are judgment, anger, and blame, while the themes of entitlement or victimhood are also often included. When you can catch an *active* compulsive reaction, you will be more likely to access and perceive the faulty beliefs at its foundation. This is important because these beliefs fuel the reactions.

Compulsive-addictive behaviors as well as compulsive-emotional reactions both contain faulty beliefs and function in a similar way. If you want to transition out of compulsive-addictive behaviors, it is essential to address both areas. This is because the compulsive-emotional reactions are most often the birthplace of the compulsive-addictive behaviors. They are both destructive. A person develops compulsive-emotional reactions when they do not know how to fully process their experiences. Sometimes they were not equipped to process on their own and a healthy role model or professional help was not available. This results in partially processed experiences, confusion, feelings of powerlessness, and layers of reactive emotion which gives rise to or brings about faulty beliefs. This creates suffering and hence a desire for distraction and escape --sometimes through compulsive-addictive. Compulsive-addictive behaviors give the illusion of relief and escape, but only on a temporary basis. Therefore, they must be endlessly repeated. With that understanding, it makes sense to address the programming at the compulsory, emotional level simultaneously with the witnessing of the compulsions that are present with addictive behaviors. However, you must be able to discern the difference between a compulsive reactive emotion and a healthy emotion.

When your emotions leave you in a state of struggle, while judging or blaming someone else or life for your circumstance, then you are in a state of unhealthy emotional reaction. Emotional reactions also occur when someone believes that they need other people to think, feel, choose, or interpret the details of life in the same manner as they do. They unconsciously want others to enable their faulty beliefs. A good example of this occurs when a person does not have as much money as they would like to have; they feel entitled when in the presence of someone with more money, and they want other people to feel guilty for not fixing their perceived problem.

Can you identify any compulsive-emotional reactions that routinely take place in your life? If so, write them down, and then contemplate to see if you can discover any assumptions or faulty beliefs that fuel the reactions.

Write down your discoveries.

_____
_____
_____
_____
_____
_____
_____
_____
_____
_____
_____
_____
_____
_____
_____
_____
_____
_____

Transitioning Beyond Your Conditioned Blueprint

_____
_____
_____
_____
_____
_____
_____
_____
_____
_____
_____
_____
_____
_____
_____

When possible, it will be beneficial to catch the compulsive-emotional reactions as they arise because any active reaction is a doorway to your subconscious mind. It is within the subconscious where all programming and reprogramming takes place. Therefore, these compulsive-emotional reactions are gifts that can help you to facilitate change. In the beginning, it will be a bit easier to address some of the less charged ones. A good place to start is with the subtle compulsive judgments that are interwoven with your thoughts throughout the day. Everyone has some of these; however, if compulsions are predominant in your life, then you will likely have many of these. Begin to make note of them throughout the day. They can sometimes appear to be very innocent when they arise. As you watch them, you will soon notice patterns of reoccurring thought within the judgments. Those are the ones where you want to put your attention. You may recognize yourself thinking things like, "People are so oblivious; that person thinks that he/she is so special; that guy thinks he's the boss; those parents don't care about their kids; look at the horrid way that person behaves or is dressed; they should be smarter than that; why don't they drive like other people?" You get the picture. There are endless examples. These are less charged, so you can much more easily catch and observe them when they arise. It is important to observe them while the emotion is active. It is the charged, active part that is the bridge to your subconscious mind. It is through the space of observing that you invite a broader understanding and insights. The insights will naturally come from deep within your consciousness as you observe the reaction. You will not be grasping for anything.

Through an ongoing practice of observing, you will more easily notice a sense of space. Once you become familiar with that space, you can also ask a question. You might ask yourself, "What belief is behind this judgment? Do I know it to be true? Did I just make that up? What am I getting out of it? Is it purposeful for me? Is it harming me or someone else?" Once you ask the question, you can let it sit in the space along with some active curiosity. Then you continue to witness. Something may or may not come at that moment. However, you can revisit it whenever it arises. Practice this as often as you can. Present one question at a time and be patient. Additional questions that you can ask about compulsive-emotional judgments are as follows: Is that any of my business? Is that my responsibility? Am I making up stories in my head about this person or situation? How did I arrive at that belief? Again, let your question sit in the space of curiosity and see if something or nothing comes to you. When you do this, you are not trying to make anything happen – you have surrendered. Let the question sit in the space that you created and see what your awareness offers. Be patient; an insight may come immediately or within hours or days. It might be something different than what you could have imagined. You will be entering into a brand-new process. When you address a compulsion on any level, you will be anchoring in a new approach that will give broad benefits. All new learning requires some degree of commitment and practice.

Practice some of this and then report back. What compulsive judgments have you noticed and what are the faulty beliefs behind them?

Write down your discoveries.

_____
_____
_____
_____
_____
_____
_____

Transitioning Beyond Your Conditioned Blueprint

_____
_____
_____
_____
_____
_____
_____
_____
_____
_____
_____
_____
_____
_____
_____
_____
_____
_____
_____
_____
_____
_____
_____
_____
_____

Now that you have had some practice witnessing and creating space with your compulsive-emotional reactions, you will be more equipped to catch the compulsive-addictive behaviors when they first arise. You can utilize the curiosity and space for self-inquiry, to recognize self-created irrational rules, irrational themes and fantasy, personalization, to reflect and gain a deeper understanding, etc. You will find that many layers of these things have been constructed at the foundation of your compulsive-addictive behaviors.

We will now proceed with your first practice run to get you acquainted with the process of addressing compulsive-addictive behaviors. These are the more heavily charged compulsions that take place within your strongest addictive behaviors. To begin, from your memory, identify a compulsive-addictive behavior that has been long-standing. Next, contemplate it. This is how you can gain a deeper understanding of any behavior. Can you see how it is routinely used as a means of escaping from personal discomfort? Now, look at the circumstances that trigger it along with the routine beliefs and the emotions that follow. Allow yourself some time to contemplate this. The contemplation will help you to identify themes, faulty beliefs, self-created rules, and will bring about an expanded understanding of the whole pattern. Can you identify any fantasy-based thinking within your compulsive-addictive behavior? Remember the fantasy-based ideas or beliefs will not be backed by facts that you directly experienced. They are assumptions, stories, and projections. Faulty beliefs are like handcuffs – they keep you trapped. As insights or facts arise, contemplate them.

Write down any new understanding and discoveries.

_____
_____
_____
_____
_____
_____
_____
_____
_____
_____
_____
_____
_____
_____
_____
_____
_____
_____
_____
_____
_____

Transitioning Beyond Your Conditioned Blueprint

As you continue to witness the compulsion, ask yourself questions about it, and then contemplate further. For example, you could ask, "How long have I been telling myself fantasy-based stories? Do I recognize any historical themes playing out in those stories?" "Am I resistant to looking at the truth of my behavior?" "Do I want to make excuses to continue while blaming others?" Now, put the themes, stories, and fantasies aside to see what remains. What is the actual truth of your experience? You will need to give yourself some time to contemplate this and be patient.

Some examples of things that you may discover could be an irrational tendency to blame other people when things go wrong, or you may feel as though you are in the wrong when others are unhappy. You may find that you are afraid of conflict, so you pretend or lie instead of being honest. You are likely to discover that many of your suffering and struggles have come about from avoiding opportunities for honest participation and inquiry.

Write down your discoveries.

Now ask, "What am I hoping to achieve through these compulsive practices, and how is it effecting my overall life?" Look at how you feel before and after the compulsive-addictive experience. Take some time to contemplate this. Write down your discoveries and any insight that has come about.

Transitioning Beyond Your Conditioned Blueprint

_____

Then ask yourself about available alternate choices and continue to contemplate. If you become aware of alternatives, contemplate them. Ask yourself, "Can I commit to myself to take action with the new choices? If not, what stops me?"

Write down any insights and new understanding.

_____

Now, reflect upon the reasons why you want to make changes and transition beyond the compulsive-addictive behavior. What would the obvious benefits be from those changes? Are you willing to make the commitment and put in the effort? As you contemplate this, you may feel some resistance or experience fear. If you are afraid or resistant, you will need to proceed courageously. Activate your warrior. To do this, you must activate your *will and fierceness*. You can make the decision to refrain from letting the fear or resistance make any decisions for you. Once you do this, you simply walk through the fear or resistance by making new choices and taking one step at a time. Contemplate to identify your first step.

Transitioning Beyond Your Conditioned Blueprint

Now, write down what you have discovered.

_____

When you recognize new options, it is important to create a plan to participate with them, so that they do not remain as a thought. They are not much good as an idea. When you sincerely set an intention and create a commitment to participate, this helps to engage your healthy *will and fierceness* for follow though. It is also beneficial to share your new commitment with someone that you trust. When you do this, the commitment is anchored in on another level of experience. As a result, it becomes more real.

With commitment, you will progressively experience greater inner space with the compulsive-addictive behaviors as well as the compulsive-emotional reactions. As a result of having more inner space, you will be able to catch them more often as they arise. Now, that you have some familiarity with this process we will proceed with more practice.

Next, identify one of your most troublesome compulsive-addictive behaviors as your new focal point. It could be the same one that you previously focused on or a different one. Ask yourself some open-ended questions and contemplate. Some example questions are: What am I trying to achieve or avoid when I engage with this compulsion? What is it doing for me? Does it cause harm or create limitations in my life? What beliefs surround it? Do I feel resistant to look at it or change it? In what ways do I protect this behavior? Do I blame others for my behavior? Do I pretend that it is not there? Why do I want to change it? Can I commit to new choices for change? If I have resistance to change, then what emotions and beliefs are fueling the resistance?

You can contemplate any number of these questions; however, focus on only one at a time and be patient with the process. Stay with this process until you are confident that you have gained an understanding of your behavior. You can practice at length or for shorter intervals throughout the day over a period of days or even weeks. For progress to take place, you must be committed and vigilant in this practice.

Remember, when you contemplate, you will not be getting drawn into any internal fantasy-based story or drama. You are not the story; you are presence. If you get distracted from witnessing, then bring your focus back, and activate your curiosity again. Remember to let your question sit in the space of active curiosity. If insights arise, contemplate them so that they become anchored.

Write down any knew understanding or discoveries.
_____
_____
_____
_____

Transitioning Beyond Your Conditioned Blueprint

As you gain an understanding of the hidden dimensions within each compulsion, you will realize that the strength of the compulsion is gradually diminishing. You will discern fantasy from fact, while gaining some sense of trust through the courageous effort that you apply with each step toward change. Understanding is essential for a change of behavior to take place. When you understand, then you have a position of stability, and your options become more apparent. To reach understanding you must be honest with yourself and acknowledge the facts as they exist in the present situation. Through acceptance, you will more clearly perceive personal responsibility, available choices, and access courage for making more new choices and ongoing changes. Without this, it will be very difficult or impossible to create personal transformation. Discovery of truth will happen in layers. It is progressive – your ongoing practice will reflect this.

If you have not yet learned a process for creating change, you may experience some resistance toward honesty. Do you feel yourself resisting the option to be honest with any habitual or compulsive situation? If so, write down your experience along with your understanding of the struggle.

_____
_____
_____
_____
_____
_____
_____
_____
_____
_____
_____
_____
_____
_____
_____
_____
_____
_____
_____
_____
_____
_____
_____
_____
_____
_____
_____

Transitioning Beyond Your Conditioned Blueprint

If you have resistance toward honesty, know that it is made up of a judgment toward change, fear of the unknown, and a desire for the familiar. You must accept that you are the one in charge of yourself – not the resistance. Do not give it any power by going along with it. For greater clarity and an anchoring of truth, contemplate it. Also, contemplate the reasons why you want to choose differently.

Write down your discoveries.

Susan V Kippen

_____
_____
_____
_____
_____
_____

Now that you have acknowledged your resistance to or anxiety about direct honest participation, you will be more able to take responsibility for the destructive effects of compulsive-addictive behavior. Are you ready to apply some courage to create change and lessen your suffering? These changes will impact the way that you experience yourself, yourself in relationships with others, and your relationship to the vast possibilities in life. To do this, you must accept what you have consciously and unconsciously created. Can you accept responsibility for your reality up to this point and dedicate yourself to moving forward with a commitment for participation, learning, and growth? You will need to participate with ongoing new choices for consistent progress. Honesty and acceptance are part of your new empowering foundation. Dishonesty creates a contracted, closed-off state of consciousness, whereas honesty is expansive. The expansiveness opens up the space in your psyche while making it easier to catch the compulsions when they occur.

When you are honest you will no longer be blocked by distorted perceptions, self-judgment, or fear. If you do have anxiety, breathe deeply in and out of your nose ten times, observe the fear so that it diminishes, and then proceed through whatever remains of it. Each time you walk through the fear, it will become less. You will be free to take steps to discover meaningful choices, to better yourself, and to receive the value from honest, direct participation in your circumstances.

To move forward you cannot have your primary focus on the past or the future. Goals and intentions are beneficial; however, the substance of life exists in the present experience of each step that you take. Contemplation can be used for gaining wisdom from the past; however, you must be primarily focused in the present while consciously navigating cause and effect, your healthy needs, true possibilities, the value of each choice that you make and the outcome of your actions. Otherwise, you will not be able to clearly comprehend where you are or your next most purposeful choice. You cannot predict where you are going;

however, you can perceive the full substance of your experience in the present moment and the best choices available in each moment. You will learn to be more comfortable navigating authentic needs as you go through this process.

Wherever compulsions continue to exist, vigilant practice will be required to gradually increase the space around them so that their power becomes diminished. This will change the way that you identify with them. They will be diluted and brought back to a more conscious level. You will have greater recognition of cause and effect. Every step that you take in life is brought about by a conscious or unconscious choice. The space or pause between each choice allows room for reasonable processing and integration of understanding on subconscious, conscious, and experiential levels. Options will become apparent most of the time through contemplation. However, you will not know how useful the options are until you apply them. When you find that a new choice does not work, you do not stop the process; you simply reevaluate and keep going with the next best choice.

Your progress will be varied. It will not go in straight line. If you find yourself in the grip of a strong compulsion and unable to create the space that you need for witnessing, then remember to start singing, go for a brisk walk, or step outside and become curious about what is around you in the environment. This will create a pause. If you choose to sing, then sing until you feel involved in the song, as though you are the song as it comes through you. If you step outside, take notice of the sights, sounds, smells, and sensations on your skin. Any of these practices can create some space. Once you create space, notice if the compulsion is still there. If so, you can then shift your focus into a state of observation and contemplation. Stay with this until you gain a clearer perspective of fantasy vs. fact and new options.

As you gain a greater understanding of your behavioral programming, realize alternate possibilities, and take steps for change, your confidence and courage will increase. This process cannot have a timeframe attached to it – that would be self-sabotaging. Attachment to a timeframe can also keep a person in an attached mind state. It is important to know that a new understanding of something cannot instantly change your life. You must gradually discover what any idea means for you as you take part in a step-by-step process of applying it to your life. Therefore, you must create a strong commitment for honest ongoing participation with each compulsive challenge. You must focus and be present. Proceed with your practice every day.

By now, you are probably catching some of the compulsions in the moment more often than not; however, you will still be noticing some of them after the fact. For a while this will be the case. Understanding something and knowing how to do it are two very different things. It takes time to learn something new. Whether you catch compulsions when they first appear or after the fact, it is important to contemplate them. When you realize that one has occurred after the fact, you might ask yourself, "What did it feel like when I made that automatic choice? How do I feel now? Was I aware of any possible consequence while I carried it out? If so, did my subconscious mind distort the truth to get me to act on it? In retrospect, how long did it take for rational thinking to come about?" Did a reactive feeling or belief trigger the compulsion? Am I suffering any negative consequences now? Did the fulfillment of the desire feel satisfying and sustainable, or was I already looking ahead to the next time that I might do it? Did I feel confused, angry, justified, guilty, shameful, indulgent, disappointed, or excited?

Each time you discover something, let yourself stay with the realization long enough to assimilate it on a deep level so that it becomes part of your foundational wisdom. You must own the truth of it. Also, contemplate alternative choices. Review your experience with this practice and write down your observations and discoveries.

_____
_____
_____
_____
_____
_____
_____
_____
_____
_____
_____
_____
_____

Transitioning Beyond Your Conditioned Blueprint

When you are able to catch the compulsion before it gets acted out, notice whether you perceive alternate options at the same time. If you do notice alternatives, what is the strength or weakness of them? Were you able to choose differently on the spot? Was there any resistance? Were you able to observe, contemplate, and walk through the resistance? If you were able to choose differently, how did it feel? If the charge behind the compulsion was stronger than your *will* to choose differently, did the compulsion choose for you? How did that feel? Did your *will and motivation for change* get strengthened from the disappointment of getting caught up in the compulsion? If so, did you contemplate it so that the understanding and wisdom could become anchored?

Write down your discoveries and thoughts.

With further practice and reflection, you will get better and better at this. With this understanding, now contemplate the reasons why you would like to

Transitioning Beyond Your Conditioned Blueprint

experience yourself as being fully capable of making conscious choices. It does not matter if you believe that you can or cannot do it. Contemplate it anyway. This will make it more real for you. You will become more confident and capable as you go step by step through the complete learning process. Vigilant daily participation is necessary for a full transition. Each day set some goals. *Purposeful conscious choices are an important way for you to create a bridge from the past to something new, and to create ongoing meaningful experiences.*

Compulsions satisfy superficial desires. That satisfaction is not sustainable. Compulsions cause harm to yourself and others. As you change your behavior by taking steps to embrace and implement new choices, you will create meaning, learn to trust yourself, and discover greater intimacy with yourself, others, and life. When something is meaningful, it often creates passion. The passion that comes through your own creative purposeful choices and experience will fulfill you on the deepest level. You will be naturally nurtured from passion and presence. You have the option to choose consciously or let compulsions choose for you. With some effort, you can transition beyond your conditioned blueprint.

Can you identify some purposeful choices and actions that you have already taken to facilitate a transformation beyond your conditioning? What is your experience of this? Can you identify the value?

_____
_____
_____
_____
_____
_____
_____
_____
_____
_____
_____
_____
_____

Continue to share your decisions for change with others along with your successes. This will make your commitment stronger as well as provide an opportunity to celebrate.

Know that as you proceed, your progress will not be predictable, always comfortable, or perfect. The mind can create a multitude of ideas about any possible new choices; however, this often has little to do with the actual unfolding experience. Sometimes you will be pleased, and sometimes you will not be pleased with the outcome. As you carry out a commitment to this process, your inner warrior will be activated some of the time. The warrior helps you to stay the course, maintain focus, be committed, and to take action with your intentions. At some point, you will notice that what was once a compulsion will be presented from your consciousness as a nonthreatening idea – just like any other idea. With this recognition, your motivation will build significantly. Continue to address the various types and layers of compulsions. A natural empowerment and greater presence will be your reward.

A process for transitioning compulsions into conscious choices

1. First you become aware of a compulsive-emotional reaction. The most common ones are judgment, anger, blame, and dependency. The states of entitlement or victimhood are also often involved. These two are also sometimes blended.
2. A good place to start is with the subtle compulsive judgments that are interwoven with your thoughts throughout the day. These will be less charged than other compulsions, so it will be easier to catch them when they are active.
3. When you catch an active reactionary compulsion vs. an idea of it, you will be more likely to access the faulty beliefs at the foundational level and begin to unravel it. The beliefs are the fuel behind the reactions.
4. When a judgment arises, activate your curiosity, and observe it. As you witness, ask yourself, "What are the beliefs behind this judgment?" Write them down and then contemplate them. You will find that most of them are false and were formulated due to unprocessed trauma, fragmented processing, projections, or faulty early programming.
5. When you become aware of faulty beliefs, you will likely become more curious and willing to make new discoveries. Look beyond the faulty beliefs to see if you recognize new possibilities. As you practice this, you will gain greater understanding. Space will be created around the

judgments and cumulatively benefit your process for transitioning all compulsions. Engage with this as often as you can.

6. As truths are recognized, sometimes resistance appears. When this occurs, it may be hard to proceed. To remedy this, witness the resistance, and use your curiosity to discover the faulty beliefs behind the resistance. Once the beliefs are realized, the resistance most often diminishes or dissipates. However, you may still need to engage your *will* to proceed.
7. When you feel adequately familiar with the process for creating space with the compulsive-emotional reactions, then it will be time to practice with a more highly charged compulsive-addictive behavior.
8. Identify a compulsive-addictive behavior and the underlying beliefs that do not serve you. You must accept responsibility for the present state of your life and commit to changing it. Set your intention to catch the compulsions as they arise.
9. Initially, you will often only see the compulsive-addictive behaviors after they have already played out. However, you can use your witnessing ability and curiosity to contemplate them anyway. As you recall the compulsions, witness the details as they unfold in your memory. Through in-depth inquiry and contemplation, you will recognize faulty beliefs and gain greater understanding.
10. Each day set some goals from the basis of where you are in your immediate experience. When you set your intention and apply yourself to challenge the compulsions, you will be strengthening and anchoring your *will* and option of choice. Each day you will do your best; yet you will not know what your best is until the day is done.
11. Accept the fact that the process will not proceed in a straight line. It will zig and zag. You will have setbacks and progress. Learning will come from all of it.
12. Sometimes it will be possible to go back and modify an outcome by taking responsibility for an unconscious choice after a compulsive act. As you proceed, you can extract wisdom through recognition of truth and possibly apply it in your next step. Beware of any old tendency to blame or distort the truth. You must choose to participate with honesty and responsibility for what you create.

13. Next, you will periodically catch the compulsive behaviors when they arise and see alternate choices at the same time. You may feel afraid of making new choices. The fear may be connected to a false or real sense of shame over the possibility of being wrong or not knowing. Real shame may come from the choice to avoid responsibility. False shame may come from projected self-judgment around the idea of failing. It is common for people with compulsions to feel trapped when they do not immediately know the answers. Consider that you have a right to not know, to make mistakes, to discover, and to learn more. Every time you do not know, it's a doorway for learning more and growing.
14. Do your best to witness and contemplate any inner struggles or unpleasant emotions before they transition into a compulsion. Seek to see more than what you think you already know. As you do this, you will gain greater understanding and have a natural awareness of yourself that continues to evolve. New possibilities will be realized.
15. Resistance may arise toward any part of the process; none the less, witness it, contemplate it, use your *will*, and walk through it. As you do this, you will be taking power away from the fear and judgment. You will be creating more space with the whole experience. These are necessary steps. You are in charge.
16. Your actions may feel unnatural; yet you acknowledge the value of each choice as you make it along with any new outcome or discoveries. Do this each time you make a new choice. It is very important for anchoring this new approach into your subconscious. You are learning how to be in a new process.
17. Celebrate all of your efforts, even when the outcome is not what you hoped.
18. Keep practicing. At some point, you will catch the compulsions more often than not, and you will more consistently redirect your experience with purposeful choices. Purposeful choices have meaning; they are not based on desires. As you go along, you gain more confidence.
19. Continue to contemplate your experiences as a daily practice. Be curious and relaxed about it instead of too serious. Too much seriousness will

lead you into doubt, judgment, and resistance. Seriousness can also keep you in a mind dominant state.
20. As you make progress, there will be times when your subconscious gets tricky with the presentation of the old compulsions. They may come up with diminished strength and seem harmless. Sometimes people get fooled into participating with an old choice because they personally feel stronger and wiser while the old choice feels weaker. Do not let yourself be fooled. If you engage, the old choice can be refueled to become a compulsion again. Your history will always be there, so it is possible for it to be re-energized into an overpowering, compulsive-addictive pattern again. Once you engage to the point where it becomes a habit, the compulsive state will be reactivated. This is the point where many people relapse into their old ways, whether it be an addiction to being right, to anger, or to alcohol. If you become seduced by the old choice and it becomes routine, the history could take you back to a self-sabotaging place of confusion, fragmented processing, and overwhelm. If this happens, know that it is sometimes part of the process. If that is the case, you can still engage your *will* and *fierceness* to say no to the shadow of the desire. Remind yourself of your history and why it was unhealthy for you as well as what is purposeful for you in the present. You will then move forward again.
21. Keep a log for documenting your experiences. Make note of the steps that you take, the discoveries you make, your setbacks, new knowledge, and your overall progress. Describe your experiences in detail. This would include your discoveries, struggles, understanding, intentions, what you witness within – unconscious and conscious choices, levels of desire, the strength of your *will* when saying no and redirecting your focus, mind created fantasy, realized truth, etc. This will help you to reinforce understanding and anchor your new process.
22. On a daily basis, continue to accept responsibility for creating your life; witness your inner experience, contemplate, practice, learn, participate, and grow.

Because the mind cannot preconceive the actual outcome of any choice, the results from each step will often be different than what you anticipated or hoped would happen. It is helpful to let go of rigid expectations and proceed with curiosity and an open mind. No matter what comes, negotiate your possibilities, and keep moving forward. The period needed to make permanent changes often depends upon the length of time that you have lived with the compulsions. Creating a committed practice of participation with curiosity, space making, witnessing, contemplation, action taking, acknowledgement of truth, acceptance, and patience are keys to your transformation and success. At times, you may have to engage your inner warrior so that you stay steadfast with your commitment.

-13-

What is my inner warrior and how do I participate with that part of me?

Your inner warrior is expressed as a courageous, stable, anchored presence within you that supports your ability to stay the course with focused determination. It is also a fierce protector that acts with courage and confidence. Your actions take place without force. The confusion of chaos cannot touch this warrior; there is an onward movement through whatever challenge is present. At times, this force will carry you through the greatest difficulties of your life. Initially, you may only be able to recognize your warrior as a protective part of you. As you become healthier, your warrior mode will be more recognizable. Sometimes if a mode of functioning is given a name and a framework to perceive it through, then it becomes more accessible. However, the experience itself is not limited by the name or framework.

It is likely that you already recognize your warrior from past situations when you were in an unsafe situation, protected another person, or even when you witnessed someone else addressing injustices toward other people or animals. This fiercely anchored assertiveness is also sometimes needed when learning something new, navigating a new situation, or to maintain the course with a purposeful goal, a deadline, a work project, or to stay focused in personal growth. Have you experienced your warrior actively taking charge in some way in your life?

If so, write down the details.

When your warrior is unbalanced or displaced, it can be a destructive force within you. It will work to keep you fiercely stuck in resistance, rebellion, and a desire for control that will undermine your ability to be curious and participate freely. It can be seen in situations when a person attempts to force an outcome with the use of anger. It will be displayed as chaotic fierceness. A self-sabotaging display of the fierceness can be recognized when a person acts out in an

Transitioning Beyond Your Conditioned Blueprint

unconscious, reactive manner. This is when the warrior is inside out. As a result of the consciousness being taken over by the unbalanced warrior you may experience fearfulness, anger, resentment, blame, judgment, jealousy, envy, competitiveness, powerlessness, and fantasy filled projections. You may have difficulty taking your goals beyond your mind – beyond a concept state.

If your inner warrior exists in an unhealthy state, it is important that you recognize it, take responsibility for what is happening, and make choices to transition this powerful mode of functioning into a purposeful, conscious, supportive aspect of self. Have you experienced an unhealthy inner warrior sabotaging your life? If so, write down the details of your experience.

Then contemplate it and write down any new discoveries.

_____
_____
_____
_____
_____
_____
_____
_____
_____
_____
_____
_____
_____
_____
_____
_____
_____
_____
_____
_____
_____
_____
_____
_____
_____
_____

Susan V Kippen

_____
_____
_____
_____

Through your inner observation and contemplation, it is important that you recognize how your inner warrior is expressing *will* and *fierceness*. The essence of *will* is an inner strength – a steady, focused attention. It is present in commitment, stubbornness, or resistance. It can be activated consciously or unconsciously. *Fierceness* can be recognized by an intensity of motivation and determination. It is the fuel that activates choice. In difficult times, the warrior supports total undistracted presence along with the focus for evaluating your best choice and course of action.

If the inner warrior is unhealthy, you will be stuck, and struggling with resistance and fear. Or you may compulsively lash out toward others with judgment, aggressive force, anger, or blame. To change this, you need to recognize what the essence of *will* and *fierceness* feel like. You can utilize the powerful stance of the *will* and the fiery determination of *fierceness* to direct your intentions. If you discover a faulty belief that is interfering with the effective use of your *will* and *fierceness,* then contemplate it. In this way you will gain a greater understanding and see options for transcending the obstacle. You must accept responsibility for what you see. Once you realize what healthy *will* and *fierceness* look like, you can engage these tools to empower your participation with purposeful choices. Following are some examples of warrior behavior.

In situations of disaster, whether personal or global, you will witness others taking focused, determined warrior action to address the needs of others. If a flood occurs, people will come together to rescue, house, feed, clothe, and tend to the needs of others. In the case of a fire, one person may go and rescue another. When a whale becomes beached, a community may come together to assist the animal back into the ocean. If you are under a deadline at work or in school to finish a project, at some point, you accept the responsibility, stay focused with the goal, and get it done. If you are doing something that you like such as an art project or learning something new, your warrior may be expressed through your commitment, passion, and steadfast participation. A committed stance is taken in each situation. However, it is not rigid; it is flexible.

Transitioning Beyond Your Conditioned Blueprint

When the warrior is used in a destructive manner, you may witness someone who is resistant to speaking up for themself when they are being controlled or bullied. Perhaps a man is married to a woman who controls all his choices. He has lost sight of his confident fierceness and choice-making capabilities. Instead of changing his situation, he stays put; he is internally angry while blaming the abuser. His *will* and *fierceness* cycle through fantasy scenarios of escape in his mind instead of enabling him to act. In another instance, a person may habitually make mistakes. When the mistakes are pointed out, this individual may become fearful, lash out, and fiercely blame others instead of listening, accepting responsibility, contemplating the problems, and using the opportunity to learn, discover something new, and participate differently. In a work situation, when a person does not like their job, they may go to work and feel like a victim instead of confidently looking for a new job or adapting to doing the best that they can with the situation at hand. Healthy *will* and *fierceness* can help a person to meet the moment while having a sense of purpose or adventure instead of drudgery.

You will all encounter many situations that are not ideal; however, you will still be required to participate. When this is the case, it is beneficial to engage your warrior. With focused, committed participation, purposeful choices are made without any intent to dominate, control, compete, convince, resist, or force anything. Instead, you embrace each step and earnestly participate. If you let resistance set in, then you will be participating with a barrier that creates a feeling of drudgery or being trapped. A clean relationship with the moment will be lost. When you commit yourself to the moment, it will not be possible to experience yourself as a victim.

Your best example of how to participate on this level often already exists within you. Some people can function best as a warrior for the benefit of others. You will see this when one person fearlessly, confidently defends someone who appears to be powerless. It is present when you are committed to overcoming a personal obstacle. It may also be recognized in a situation when you are learning something new or wholeheartedly defending a cause. It could also involve a situation where you are called to action to troubleshoot something.

However, as previously mentioned, sometimes it is disguised in the form of stubbornness or resistance when a person defends unhealthy behavior or an imagined scenario. The person would still be using their *fierceness* and *will* to take a stand; however, it would be destructive rather than purposeful.

Can you recognize any times when you have stepped into your warrior role – either healthy or unhealthy? Write down the details.

Transitioning Beyond Your Conditioned Blueprint

_____
_____

Now, take what you recognize of your warrior self, intentionally activate it, and apply this approach to a purposeful choice in an area where you have been stuck. Once you take action for the first step, contemplate the outcome of that step so that you can gauge what your next step or choice will be, then continue in this process.

Helpful steps for engaging your inner warrior

1. Sometimes you will need to engage your inner warrior when you are feeling stuck or struggling. When you realize this, you need only to shift your focus to transform your experience with the help of this innate part of you.
2. To begin, contemplate to recognize where you are having a struggle or in what way you are feeling stuck or powerless. Through inner observation, seek to understand how you are keeping yourself stuck. It may be from fear, a faulty belief, a sense of entitlement, a judgment of self or another person, or a lack of understanding. A struggle can also occur from processing for others instead of for yourself, from resistance, procrastination, self-suppression though a victim role, dependency on someone else, attachment to maintaining a false sense of control by doing the same thing over and over, or something else. When you unconsciously choose in these ways, you will feel trapped, stuck, or like a victim of someone else or your own circumstances. The longer you participate unconsciously, any reactivity that you have will gradually increase, leading to greater perceptions of disempowerment. Once you see the truth, you will see that you are doing this to yourself. You may need some assistance from your warrior to transition.
3. Based on what you have learned, recall a situation where you utilized your warrior in a healthy or unhealthy manner. Through your recall, get a sense of the active experience of *will* and *fierceness – not just the idea of it*. Transfer the experience of this warrior stance into your present

situation. Utilize it to engage your focus and motivation to act and stay present.

4. To make the transition, you must accept responsibility for the complete process of changing your experience. Next, contemplate your possibilities and remain present whether the situation is pleasant or unpleasant. Do not look for options from a wishful or reactive basis, avoidance, or rigid desire. Decide to be courageous rather than fearful. You must transition through each obstacle courageously with the best available choices. If you choose to stay in a fearful place, then you will not engage your healthy warrior or learn anything new. Committed determination without force supports passionate fierceness.

5. Where there is fear, acknowledge it, and then use your fierce determination and *will* to walk through it. Do not wait for the fear to go away. Each time you need to take another step but have resistance, remember to recall the warrior role from any past situation, get a feel for it, and then transfer it into the foundation of your actions when making new choices. Every step brings a new variation of experience. You will make ongoing discoveries, develop greater personal trust and confidence, and the fear will diminish. It can eventually disappear.

6. Accept the fact that you cannot know or predict your experiences. You must decide to courageously trust in your ability to make the best choices available in the moment and take the most appropriate actions for each situation as it unfolds. Know that your choices are not finite. With any plan or goal, you will discover that there are often more steps than you anticipated and more to learn than you could have imagined. The mind cannot perceive an exact unfolding process. Be mentally and emotionally prepared for this.

7. Embrace the experience of not knowing. Much of life is about not knowing and making discoveries. Know that all choices lead to more choices. With each conscious decision there is more life rather than less life.

8. When you let go of the fearful fight, judgment, and resistance, you allow *grace* to be present in your unfolding experiences.

Transitioning Beyond Your Conditioned Blueprint

9. Remember that the development of personal trust, fulfillment, and harmony requires participation.
10. If you are having trouble maintaining your focus or continue to get stuck, once again, recall a situation from your past when you effectively carried out the warrior mode. Then alternate your focus between this and the present situation which involves the struggle. This process strengthens your ability to observe and creates space while diminishing the reactivity. As you create the space and continue to observe, the struggle gradually dissipates and is eventually gone. Keep alternating your focus back and forth until you get some results. This can be effective in one 30-minute session, or, if you have a tremendous amount of resistance, you may have to practice it off and on for several days. Continue until you feel some degree of change.

Chapter Five

Overcommitting Yourself Can Block Authentic Experience and Negatively Affect Your Overall Health

-14-
The importance of having space between responsibilities and activities

The space that you do or do not have between your activities and responsibilities will affect the quality of your physical and psychological/emotional experience.

As you embark upon a path of greater self-awareness, it is important to pay attention to your lifestyle. If you want to experience space with your thoughts and emotions, you must have space between your day-to-day experiences. All aspects of your life are intertwined to some degree.

If a person is consistently overscheduled, then they are diminishing their possibility to have inner space, to contemplate and make sense of life, and regenerate. If this becomes a long-term habit, the regimented approach and self-imposed rules of a busy schedule can take over to dictate what will be a surface level of seemingly predictable experience. The busyness can create the illusion of control and perfection. This approach can become compulsive. When this is the case, the person will not easily access or perceive the unplanned, spontaneously everchanging level of human experience – the non-doing state. A state of presence and surrender from planned activities is necessary for this to take place. When someone is mind dominant, they are partially subdued – held captive by the regimented approach and an agenda mindset. Do not let ideas of what you think *should be* override your innate need to just *be* some of the time. Just because you can do something does not mean that it is good for you. The masculine nature of behavior governs planning, organizing, troubleshooting, taking action as well as formulating and fulfilling the ideas within goals. Alongside that, the feminine experiential level of self is expressed through stillness, space, receptivity, creativity, passion, spontaneity, and the ability to just be, etc. To maintain stability in health along with inner peace and fulfillment, you must have balance between both parts of the self. Commitment to responsibilities need to be interwoven with intervals of free-flowing personal experience.

When you are mind-dominant for an extended period, it will be difficult to access deep authentic experience. Therefore, you will not have the space in your psyche to perceive what fits or does not fit for your true needs, sense of purpose, or well-being. Your creativity and insight will be subdued or blocked. You will become more serious – less open. This will lead to black and white thinking, which reinforces in an overactive mind. The mind alone cannot perceive authentic process – it only perceives ideas of things. This is because it cannot surrender to the unknown or the experiential unfolding of life. It wants to be in charge and arrange your experience in a predictable conceptual manner. It functions on ideas, which is different than the experiential unfolding level. You need both the mind and free flowing experience working together.

When you push yourself beyond what is natural, your body will be in a state of adrenaline dominance. The body does not know the difference between pleasant and unpleasant stress. Even when you think that all your tasks are fulfilling, there is a point where your pace will become too much, and your body will respond accordingly. For instance, if you load up your schedule with professional work, household tasks, social visits, personal interests, and fitness requirements with no space in between these activities, you will not properly regenerate or take in the wisdom of life. Processing will likely take place on a surface level. As a result, you will create stress on physical, mental, emotional, and spiritual levels. When this takes place over time, there is a cascade effect.

The unending layers of responsibility, the desire to achieve and acquire, along with efforts to rationalize or ignore unresolved inner turmoil will pile up and affect your experience of self on every level. At some point, you will not feel safe because you are only partially present. You will often feel an ongoing void, but you will be unlikely to recognize why the void is there. Most of the time you will not understand what you need because you will not have access to a state of presence or the space for contemplation and deep processing. You may feel anxiety or confusion as you seek safety through the illusion of predictability with overdoing and controlling behaviors. A sense of urgency will lead you from one activity to the next, with no space in between. In the extreme this will produce paranoia. When your situation reaches this point, a mental/emotional breakdown is possible. People are often not aware of what is happening until they find themselves in a state of complete overload.

The constant flow of adrenaline can produce fatigue, physical illness, sleep problems, digestive issues, forgetfulness, feelings of being overwhelmed, dullness, depression, anxiety, anger, or hopelessness. Chemically, the body's ability to produce the hormone GABA decreases which means that your ability to relax, sleep, and digest food is diminished. As your histamine levels increase, you may develop allergies and food sensitivities. It is possible for the physical body to be worn down to the point where it can no longer properly regenerate.

It is common practice for adrenaline-dominant people to seek help through prescription drugs, psychological guidance, herbs, acupuncture, yoga, special diets, cognitive therapy, etc.; however, these things will only bring minimal and temporary relief. The foundational problem of *overscheduling with the resulting lack of space* must be addressed first. Then other forms of help will be much more effective.

Does any of this correlate with any of your own experiences? If so, write down what you have learned.

_____
_____
_____
_____
_____
_____
_____
_____

Contemplate your experience to discern which of your activities are the most purposeful and necessary. Then simplify and restructure your daily approach so that you have some space between the activities. This will be your first exercise to restructure and simplify your daily experience. A second one will come later.

Write down what you have identified.

Transitioning Beyond Your Conditioned Blueprint

_____

Overcommitting your time can lead you to feel overwhelmed and trapped. When you are overwhelmed, it is important to know why it is happening and how to transition out of it.

When you are overwhelmed, you have lost your ability to be present and prioritize, keep a clean focus, and make purposeful, healthy choices. You will have lost your sense of space. Rather than fully participating in the moment, there will be judgment or some resistance toward your present reality and a desire to instantly step into an imaginary end result or comfortable scenario. Your sense of surrender and trust are not intact. You cannot perceive a process for transitioning out of your present struggle or unhappiness. A present moment process is your bridge from suffering to well-being. A sense of space must be created to establish room for a conscious process. This process begins as you participate with curiosity and contemplation. You will then gain understanding, make discoveries and new choices, contemplate further, make more discoveries and so on, until you make a transition.

To create space in this type of situation, you must first pause. Then ask yourself a question about your immediate priorities. Once you identify them, you can take the first step for creating change while accepting that you will probably need more than one step to complete your immediate goal and then transition your overall situation. Keep your focus on each step rather than looking at everything that is overwhelming you. Just let go of everything else for the moment as though that one detail is all that matters. This will anchor you in the moment. Between each step maintain your curiosity to gain clarity for the next step. Solutions and completion often come after taking many steps; however, you can only be present and effective in one step at a time.

When prioritizing your choices, if everything is of equal importance, then it often makes sense to choose the most challenging thing first because that is where you will feel the greatest reward. This will likely address your largest area of resistance as well. Instead of trying to get rid of the resistance, simply acknowledge it, and walk through it. Sometimes it is useful to remember something difficult that you were able to accomplish at an earlier time and associate your previous success with the step that you are taking now. The subconscious is more likely to ease into accepting the choice when you make this type of association. For example, you might say to yourself, "Just like I was able to apply myself and learn how to cook or paint my house, I can apply myself to this task right now." As you make progress, remember to acknowledge and celebrate it mentally and emotionally. This anchors self-confidence and motivation. Once you complete one priority, reevaluate to see what comes next through contemplation, and then take your first step in the new priority. Do not let your mind dwell on everything that needs your attention, or you will likely become overwhelmed again. Stay present in each step and remember to pause between each one. Once the feeling of being overwhelmed clears, you will probably want to evaluate to the reasons why you have been attached to the activities and responsibilities that have filled up your time. A foundation of understanding is important for creating a new plan of simplification.

You will find that you can always eliminate or adjust some activities and perceived responsibilities so that you can have space. Your life may depend upon it. Perhaps you can delegate some tasks to family members, friends, or coworkers. Also, contemplate your situation to identify your healthy limits, and then practice saying *no*. If you feel guilty about this, then ponder your beliefs about personal responsibilities and those that relate to others. Do not take on responsibility for the perspectives and reactions in other people. Create a boundary by letting go of judgment and responsibility toward them.

Instead, be curious and seek to understand other people. This may seem difficult at first. You may have to courageously walk through some fear and resistance. Ask for help when you need it, and don't try to figure everything out by yourself. Sometimes the habit of overexerting yourself by doing too much comes from trying to be perfect. If you tend to do this, then adjust your expectations, and recognize your limits. This does not mean that you are any less capable or that you have failed. It is an opportunity for you to let go of self-created rules, allow new experiences into your life, and learn something new.

Sometimes perfectionism can be an aspect of a co-dependency. When this is the case, a person feels responsible for satisfying the needs of others without regard for their own. If this is you, it is likely that you will be resistant to asking for help and pretend that your needs do not exist. You may also find yourself saying yes when you want to say no. With this pattern of behavior, you may believe that you are wrong to have your own needs or be afraid to feel vulnerable with others. An unrealistic responsibility toward others is often fueled by a fear of rejection or false guilt which fills and closes off the space you need to be present. When this occurs, it will be very difficult for you to process your individual experience. In this case, it will be helpful for you to create some physical space to contemplate your beliefs, access a clearer understanding of yourself and the situation. Then make new purposeful choices.

Also, if you have created any timeframes for yourself, loosen them up or eliminate them if they are not truly necessary. Artificial timelines put tremendous pressure on you and create a feeling of urgency that will keep you a step ahead of your experiences.

Now, contemplate what you have learned so far about your tendency to take on too many activities and responsibilities. Remember to be curious and receptive. Take a few minutes. Then ask yourself some open-ended questions. Let yourself relax in the pause that is created with each question. Examples of questions might be, "How long have I been functioning in a state of overdoing? Have I felt trapped or claustrophobic during this time period? Do I feel a void or flatness inside? Is there a sense of needing to escape? Have I habitually done this throughout my life? If not, when did it start? What emotions and beliefs have been driving it? Do I know how to let go of an attachment to being in charge? Can I break some of my own rules to challenge myself and my relationship with the habit of overcommitting?

Write down your discoveries.

Transitioning Beyond Your Conditioned Blueprint

_____
_____
_____
_____
_____
_____
_____
_____
_____

   Evaluate how much space is available in your day. Each day reflect upon the reasons why you perceive something to be a priority, and ask yourself if it is true or not? Simplify by letting go of some things on your to do list. To save time on a practical level do your food shopping once a week; plan to cook some meals ahead and freeze them. If your clothes are not dirty, wear them again. Also, look at the little things that fill up space. Then eliminate what is not of value. Are you compulsively spending time on the computer? How often are you engaged in unnecessary phone calls or texting? Does gossip or drama-based conversation with others take up your time? Do imaginary scenarios take up space in your psyche? Eliminate what is not truly meaningful, and consciously choose to *just be,* to contemplate, and allow yourself to be nurtured by the stillness of life. If you do not consciously create space between responsibilities, you will end up seeking it through unconscious, compulsive, superficial distractions.
   These unconscious compulsive distractions might include browsing the internet, playing video games, online shopping, watching TV, consuming alcohol, using drugs, overeating, indulging in porn, obsessing with internal dramas, or gossiping. These things create the illusion of space through a temporary distraction. They appear to temporarily fulfill a need without solving the overall problem. They will most often add more stress because they are not part of a solution.
   In your free time, you may need to rest or have fun. It is important to consciously decide what is meaningful and purposeful. When you are present on a deep experiential level, you will be naturally nurtured through the state of presence. You will also be more likely to access true knowing, resolve, and realizations for personal growth and transformation.

Overthinking is a major obstacle to the experience of inner space. The practices of pretending, worrying, making judgments, assigning blame, and being dependent are all contributing factors to this. These behaviors can come from unfulfilled needs, fragmented processing, and personalization which leads the mind into repetitive patterns of thought. Be careful about getting stuck in a state of desire over things that cannot be. This is when your mind will make up things and lead you into a state of drama. The solution is to remain curious about yourself, others, and every situation. There is always more to discover and to be understood. Be honest with yourself and other people while accepting the best, the worst, and all the variables of each experience.

At times, when people become psychologically bogged down by life, they will unconsciously seek freedom by purging their material possessions from their living environment. They will feel good while they are doing it; however, the effects are not lasting. For instance, when a shopping addiction is present, the person sometimes learns to keep purging from their living environment for the purpose of convincing themself that they need more stuff. They are enabling themself by creating an illusion. This can reinforce denial and feed the addiction. The most effective purging needs to take place within their own consciousness. What is needed at a deep experiential level will not be accomplished with these cosmetic practices. Instead, a person must look inside of oneself rather than outside. When they apply curiosity, the door will be opened for accessing clarity and understanding so that they can clean out the internal closets. If they don't do this, then they will continue to reintroduce clutter into their environment.

At this point, you have likely identified some unconscious activities and practices that fill up your internal and external space. Contemplate your relationship with them. In what ways can you better coordinate and balance your relationship with external activities? Can you identify any habitual internal dialogues that need to be transformed? In what ways can you redirect your attention when the unhealthy dialogues become activated? Can you accept your natural healthy limits?

Contemplate your overall situation and then write down your insights.
_____
_____
_____

Transitioning Beyond Your Conditioned Blueprint

_____
_____
_____
_____
_____
_____
_____
_____
_____
_____
_____
_____
_____
_____
_____
_____
_____
_____
_____
_____
_____
_____
_____
_____
_____
_____
_____
_____
_____
_____
_____
_____
_____
_____

Now, this will be your second exercise to simplify and change your habits. Contemplate your situation to discover where you can adjust or eliminate some additional task, personal activities, or mind clutter to bring more space into your life. This process will need to be repeated periodically. As a reminder, this modification may include you asking for help, creating healthy limits with activities and interest, letting go of unrealistic expectations of perfectionism, spontaneously paying attention to your needs, letting go of dictatorial self-created rules, saying no to the unreasonable expectations of others, etc. Also, remember that you cannot predict the outcome of any experience. Remain flexible. The mind will sometimes project an alternate version of whatever is to occur and then rebel against it when the unfolding experience and outcome is different. So, beware of this, and be ready to adjust your focus and perspective as you go along.

Write down your revised plan for simplifying your circumstances, activities, and inner experience.

Transitioning Beyond Your Conditioned Blueprint

_____
_____
_____
_____

Once you have space between responsibilities and activities, it is important to stay consciously aware so that you do not fall back into old habits. Remember any previous, long-standing compulsions can get reactivated. When you notice a feeling of urgency arise about getting things done, contemplate it to discern whether it is appropriate for your current situation or not. You will have to be vigilant with this for a while. It will take time for you to get accustomed to having space and being in a non-doing state.

-15-

Familiarizing yourself with a conscious, non-doing state

This is a spontaneous state – you are in the moment. When you are in a non-doing state, it does not mean that you are not making choices or participating in an activity. You are present within the experience of the moment without having a dominant, forward agenda. Your choices are free of compulsive actions and reactions. You are present and receptive rather than chasing after something. Your happiness is not attached to the idea of finishing a task or accomplishing anything. Instead, you receive value from the overall experience which includes each step as it occurs. When you are fully present in each step, you are an embodiment of the experience as it unfolds. You are gracefully making your choices while accepting what can and cannot be. You make the most fitting choice in each moment. You are not judging the outcome of any action. Judgments will lead to reactions and compulsive thinking. Hence, a mind dominant state would block you from being curious and receptive. When the mind is dominant, it will be giving you unnecessary information, creating projections, judging, telling stories, etc. When you are in the moment, the mind will not be distracting you with any of this. You will naturally access insight, understanding, and wisdom. A sense of surrender permeates your entire experience. You will be free of all resistance.

If you at first find yourself feeling resistant and struggling to let go, then take a walk or rest for 15 minutes. You will be creating a pause to help reset your mode of functioning. As you proceed again and you are able to let go, acknowledge your success. When a person recognizes the value of something, it is easier to continue. It also helps to recognize that you are the one choosing rather than feeling like unconscious resistance or a habit is forcing you to function in a certain way.

If you continue to have difficulty being present to take new actions, you can associate each step with a familiar healthy, unattached routine from your day-to-day life. Let yourself recall a simple everyday experience that feels natural, like brushing your teeth, getting dressed, taking a walk, emptying the dishwasher, cooking, taking a shower, having a conversation, folding laundry, etc. You can take the memory of any of these experiences and associate the feeling of it with the step that you are about to take. This association helps to reinforce familiarity, gives encouragement, and can transition you into a state of presence. It can serve as a nice supportive bridge. The bridge really is the process or journey between idea and result. It is the substance of your experience. When in a spontaneous, non-doing state, you are naturally nurtured by life.

When you are present in a non-doing state, you are choosing as you go along. You are in the full experience of each situation as you make choices. You will not be a step ahead of your experience or attached to a timeframe. You are not hyper-focused on specific details. Nothing is personalized. All aspects of your experience are harmoniously blended. This process is familiar to most people when recalling pleasant activities.

Some people enjoy playing golf, cooking, gardening, playing music, making art, participating in theater, joyfully engaging with others, walking, or running. This kind of harmonious experience also takes place when a person is enjoying a pleasant vacation. This creates a natural disruption from your usual patterns, stimulates curiosity, and brings a person into the moment. When something brings joy, there is generally a complete acceptance of it. That acceptance supports curiosity, receptivity, and total presence.

Transitioning Beyond Your Conditioned Blueprint

When someone is well practiced in a presence state of awareness, it can be experienced while in the grocery store, the bank, at work, while sharing with others, taking a walk, participating in a project, or in any circumstance. When a person becomes naturally merged with the activity, an agenda-oriented state will not exist. The act of surrender and immersion creates an experience of space that is not separate from the activity.

As you practice, the experience of harmony will gradually stabilize. Be patient while becoming familiar with the experience of spontaneous participation vs. agenda-oriented participation. Patience creates space which will help you to be more aware and make the transition from a mind-dominant state to a non-doing experience.

Can you recall some examples of when you have or now routinely function in a conscious, non-doing state? You might ask yourself, "Why is this possible for me in some situations and not others? What is my mind doing or not doing? Do I experience any active curiosity or resistance? Do I recognize the experience of expansiveness or space in those situations? What does it feel like to have space while participating in my experiences?" Can I recognize how I am benefitted from a non-doing state mentally, emotionally, physically, and spiritually? Am I able to consciously shift myself from an attached state to a non-doing state? If not, then what gets in the way of it? If I am not able to be present in the moment, what is my mind doing? Have I created rules that I filter my experiences through? Now reflect upon this section. Then write down any realizations that come to you.

_____
_____
_____
_____
_____
_____
_____
_____
_____
_____

_____
_____
_____
_____
_____
_____
_____
_____
_____
_____
_____
_____
_____
_____
_____
_____
_____
_____
_____
_____
_____
_____
_____
_____
_____
_____

Contemplate all that you have written down and then ask yourself, "Am I ready to make different choices, adjust my life, and do the work that needs to be done so that I can have greater health, peace, and fulfillment?" Can you accept responsibility for changing your conditioned patterns and behaviors? It's up to you.

Steps for transitioning from an overcommitted state to a balanced experience

1. First, engage your curiosity to contemplate and understand your current lifestyle and overall situation. As you contemplate the larger

picture of your life, you will gain a greater understanding of yourself, your responsibilities, appropriate boundaries, priorities, and true possibilities vs. fantasy. Let go of perfectionism while accepting that you cannot do everything. Learn to break your own rules as well as the rules that you imagine others have placed upon you.

2. Notice when self-created rules, perfectionism, or other people's expectations are making blanket decisions for you. Choose according to your actual needs and circumstances in each situation.

3. Make new choices, as needed, instead of falling into routines or complacency with your habitual ways.

4. Pace yourself with responsibilities and goals. Accept your limits.

5. Learn to pay attention to your authentic needs while expressing yes and no honestly whether you are interacting with yourself or someone else.

6. As you gain a greater understanding of yourself and each situation, walk through your fears.

7. Do not take responsibility for any inappropriate reactions and attachments from others. Discern the difference between yourself and others. Take in what is meaningful and create boundaries when appropriate.

8. Do not let others process for you. Be mindfully present with your own experiences and needs. Then process for yourself. Other people cannot decide what is best for you.

9. Through contemplation, discern where responsibility between yourself and others begins and ends. Create boundaries as needed. Boundaries help you to define how your focus is directed as well as how you use your energy. The act of saying yes or no is natural when you are authentically present. Creating a boundary also creates a pause or a space where awareness becomes enhanced.

10. If you feel a reaction to something, contemplate it. Look at the underlying beliefs and challenge them with truth-based choices.

11. Be aware of internal drama. It will fill up your emotional, psychological, spiritual space. Say no to it and redirect your focus into something purposeful.

12. Consider whether you are overcommitted because you unconsciously wish to escape from unresolved inner turmoil. When this is the case, seek to understand and resolve the turmoil.

13. If you need support, share your experience with a healthy, objective, understanding person, or get professional medical help.

14. Do not pretend or hide yourself – be honest and authentic. Secrecy prevents honest participation with other people and your circumstances while encouraging internal drama. If you pretend, you will not have access to real options. You will be more aware of the imaginary ideas that come through reactions to your fears or judgments.

15. Get plenty of sleep so that you can regenerate.

16. Foster healthy relationships – avoid drama with others.

17. Take time to fulfill your passions which may include creative endeavors, reading, listening to music, writing, cooking, watching sports, hiking, sailing, research, etc. Take a vacation. This creates a natural disruption from your usual patterns, stimulates curiosity, and brings you into the moment.

18. Listen to music while singing out loud. This helps to balance the nervous system and aids with the production of the hormones endorphins and oxytocin. Endorphins reduce stress and improve your sense of well-being. Oxytocin enhances the experience of trust and bonding between people.

19. Spend time in nature. Let yourself experience the forest, ocean, streams, lakes, sky, and the wind without being distracted by ideas of things to do or conversation with other people.

20. Laugh a lot – see the humor in life.

For people to be balanced, they need to participate to some degree on all levels of human experience while creating the time and space to contemplate and integrate the value and wisdom of each experience. The deepest joy in life comes from being present.

-16-

Techniques for resolving anxiety when you are worried or overwhelmed

Give all of these techniques a try to see which ones work best for you. You can use them as often as needed individually or in combination.

1. First take ten deep slow breaths in and out of the nose. This will help to ground you. The slow exhale through the nostrils will support greater absorption of oxygen. Next, observe the anxiety while recognizing that it is a quality of emotion that cannot do anything to you. It is just a vibrational frequency and can only affect you if you react to it. If you do not apply any meaning to it, then it is nothing but a vibration. However, notice if you are reacting to it. If you are doing that, then make the choice to observe the reaction. It will most often diminish. Once that diminishes simply observe any remaining anxiety with curiosity. The observation naturally gives anxiety the space to process on its own and diminish. Once this occurs, you will often gain insight. Then put your focus into something purposeful. Repeat this process as needed.

2. When a quick temporary transition from anxiety is needed, do the following. Take ten deep breaths through the nose for grounding and increased absorption of oxygen. Then take a fifteen minute fast-paced walk or run. You can run inside your house or outside. When you have anxiety, there is a subconscious desire to flee. Through this process you will be convincing the subconscious mind that an escape is taking place. The anxiety will most often diminish or disappear.

3. If your circumstances allow for contemplation, observe to identify the specific worry, faulty belief, or rule that underlies the anxiety. Once you recognize the basic truth of any of these, know that they are only temporary experiences that make up a very small part of your overall experience. Your persistent focus and the meaning that you put into them makes them appear to be large. In the context of your overall life experience, they are small. Expand your perception out into the larger picture of your present experience. This means that you are

acknowledging all of the details from a position of truth while leaving out assumptions and stories. You have transitioned yourself from a micro-focus on the presumed problem into a panoramic view of your present life experience. This creates a greater sense of safety and dilutes the original experience of anxiety.

4. If you are afraid of something bad happening, acknowledge that what you imagine is not happening now, and it may never happen. You might say to yourself, "My mind has been presenting scary ideas to me. None of that is real right now, and it may never be real. What will happen in the next moment, day, week, or month is not predictable. I am in a much better position right now than what I imagined. I am safe."

Now acknowledge the real facts and available choices in your immediate situation. If you cannot identify any options of choice, simply acknowledge the need for your experience to further unfold. As it unfolds, more details will be shown to you. As you make discoveries, you will recognize more options of choice. At this point, you will likely be able to transition yourself from a fear state to an active state of curiosity. The curiosity will support an ongoing discovery process. Once you redirect yourself through this present moment process, you will find yourself to be much better off than what your imagination was leading you to believe.

-17-

Instructions for a walking meditation

This walking meditation can be used for developing a present moment awareness and experience of internal space while at the same time, supporting the balance between the mind and the experiential level of self.

This simple method involves participation with your five senses - sight, hearing, taste, touch, and smell. A meditative practice helps to free the mind from taking up a dominant role. With this practice, the mind is present to acknowledge details; however, that is as far as it goes. The rest is experiential. At first, it is best to do this out in nature during quiet walks so that you become familiar with the process. Then you can put it to the test when you are at home or out and about.

As you walk, pay attention to any stimuli that are coming through your senses. There may be the feel of the wind on your skin, a scent in the air, a sound from a bird, the warmth or coolness of the air on your skin, an overall sensation from your whole experience, or the visual brilliance of a color or shape or texture. Start with one sensation, such as the rhythmic movement of your feet as you walk along. Then shift your focus to notice the sounds of the birds or feel the sun on your skin. Continue shifting your focus from one sensory point to another. You may have to consciously pause and then refocus if you are not accustomed to noticing in this way. Let your focus alternate between the various senses while lingering briefly with each focal point. Practice until it feels natural for you to experience through your senses. This goes beyond the thinking mind. As you keep participating in this way, the mind becomes less active. This has the potential to eventually lead you to a state of synchronization between the mind and the experiential level. There will be a spaciousness within that has no boundaries. With practice, the appearance of inner duality disappears; there is a sense of oneness with All. You can practice this anywhere.

-18-

Instructions for a regenerative meditation

The next meditation is for regenerating your body from burnout or injury. It is a body focused, experiential practice. Energy follows unattached focus. Therefore, when you focus inwardly, energy naturally flows into the body to repair and recharge you.

1. This can be done anytime during the day, before bedtime, or when you wake up at night. To begin, find an undisturbed place where you can sit or lay down for 20 minutes or longer. Close your eyes while bringing your focus inward. Put your attention on a body sensation that stands out. Begin with the most obvious body feeling.

2. This may be tightness, tingling, pain, heaviness, or any other type of body sensation. As you do this, simply notice what is there. Do not look for something that is not there or try to make anything be a certain way.

3. Your focus is relaxed – not attached. If you are serious, then you are primarily in the mind, and you will remain attached. Do not analyze what you feel or create stories about it. There is also no like or dislike of your experience.

4. As you proceed, other body feelings will call to your attention. As this happens, let your focus naturally shift to the new sensation. Stay with the process as it fluctuates and changes. Sensations will arise and fade away. If you have aches and pains, they will diminish. Tightness will loosen up and energy will flow more freely.

5. Do not let your mind interfere with the process by projecting any expectation, judgment, or impatience. Try not to react to or personalize what you perceive – no drama. If drama or a story appears, redirect your focus back to the sensation. You should have no agenda. You are simply in the experience as presence. The experience of presence is that of spaciousness and well-being.

6. At a certain point, you will feel strengthened to some degree and will know that it is time to shift your experience into something else. You can resume your daily activities or go to sleep.

Note – I discovered this practice while meditating during the time when I suffered from the concussion. It was very effective for regenerating my brain function as well as relieving back pain.

Take some time to become familiar with all that has been discussed in this section. You must develop a personal practice of inner witnessing to open up more internal space. Once you can do that, the space supports more contemplation, discovery, balanced choices, and overall enrichment. As you bring more space to your everyday personal solitary experiences, you will notice that some aspects of this practice will naturally transition into your outer experiences with other people. However, you will still have to deal with all of your everyday triggers that take you out of a state of presence. One of the most common reactions for all people is personalization.

People tend to personalize; however, they don't understand what they are doing, so they don't recognize it to be an obstacle or know how to change it.

Chapter Six
Common Obstacles to Self-Awareness

-19-
How can I recognize it when I am personalizing?

When you are personalizing you are likely to find yourself believing that someone else is responsible for the way that you feel and believing that their perceptions can compromise you. You will likely feel that they can make you be or not be a certain way and that this person should think or choose in the same way that you wish them to participate or proceed. There is generally a strong attachment to what the other person is doing or not doing, along with the perception that they are bad, wrong, adversarial, or unfair. Your reactions will also suggest the idea that this person can perceive your needs and is capable of and responsible for acting in accordance with your personal understanding of a situation. You may believe that they are consciously choosing to do the wrong thing; therefore, they are doing something to you.

When this happens, you will not have confidence in yourself. Instead, you will have moved into an inferior position, having created a state of psychological/emotional dependency on the other person. You will feel that you cannot be okay, unless the other individual comes around to seeing things in the way that you do. Your personal anchor becomes uprooted; however, you will not see that this was your own doing – facilitated by your personal beliefs. Your own internal conflict will produce a deluge of emotions. You may feel judgment toward yourself or the other person, competitiveness, resentment, defensiveness, self-righteousness, envy, inferiority, anxiety, anger, sadness, or something else. Anger through indignation will sometimes make you feel more confident; but this will eventually just drag you down further. It is false confidence which is dependent upon the other person being wrong or feeling bad. This will also lead to defensiveness. When you feel defensive, it will be anchored in a belief that you must fight to protect or keep your own experience, even though it is there and will always be within you — before, during, and after any situation that plays out. It is the belief that someone else or your own choices can decide that you are bad, wrong, or maybe *can't be authentic* that drives the defensiveness.

The next reactive step that takes place is often a resistance toward openly sharing or discovering anything else about the person with whom you had the original conflict. A misconstrued, distorted, or unspoken conflict can turn into avoidance, internal stories, or a bad attitude toward others. Other people may be unaware of your thoughts and feelings. They may be confused and think that you are troubled, you simply don't like them, or that you are a mean person. They may also be personalizing you.

Without a willingness to communicate, to remain open and curious during interactions, and to have compassion for oneself and the other people, no understanding or solutions can come. However, the subconscious will still need solutions. When there is an aversion to being honest and present, to negotiating possibilities within yourself or with someone else, the mind will try to create a solution or a way out of the experience through blame. Out of desperation an ongoing drama will be created. This most often occurs compulsively. Meanwhile you have no awareness of it being a drama. Nor do you recognize an alternate way to process your experience. This drama can happen as self-contained internal turmoil, or you may draw others into the drama and personalization with you. When you get others to engage with you on this level, you amplify the experience of a victim role. Everyone involved takes on a powerless role to some degree. Multi-layered participation in fantasy will be the result when details are taken from the original experience and offered up for an emotional replay with others. When others join in and agree, with your interpretation, you might feel a false sense of resolution on a temporary basis, but it is only an illusion. The original problem will still exist. Additionally, you develop a dependency on others to agree with your story. For a solution to come about, the original players must directly interact with a sincere effort on both sides to gain understanding and resolution, or you must look inward to discover your own faulty beliefs.

Sometimes it is not possible or helpful to engage with the original players. Then you must accept the reality and create the appropriate boundaries. The exact specifics of the boundary will depend upon the situation. It may mean that you do not participate in a certain way with the person or engage only in certain conversations. If you have had repeated unhealthy interactions, then you know what the possibilities are. If there is no perceivable value in remaining connected to the person, then you stop contact with them. To pretend is to be submissive to their behaviors.

Can you recognize any recent or past instances of personalization with another person or situation? You would likely have created fantasy or drama in response to it, instead of seeking to understand and resolve the conflict through honest, direct inquiry or acceptance and the creation of boundaries.

Write down your example.

_____
_____
_____
_____
_____
_____
_____
_____
_____
_____
_____
_____
_____
_____
_____
_____
_____
_____

Transitioning Beyond Your Conditioned Blueprint

Can you separate the fabricated details from the actual details? The imagined particulars are the ones that are used to formulate a dramatic interpretation and suggest that harm is being done to you. The real facts are the ones that you directly experienced. They do not include any embellishments or assumptions.

Write down the fabricated details.

Next, write down the real details. These are the ones that you experienced in a direct manner. They will not include assumptions or long-standing beliefs.

Transitioning Beyond Your Conditioned Blueprint

Now, contemplate what you have discovered thus far to identify any faulty beliefs. Write them down, and then look at whether you are willing to let go of them in order to discover more, from within yourself and from another person.

Write down your detailed thoughts about this.

Transitioning Beyond Your Conditioned Blueprint

_____
_____
_____
_____
_____
_____
_____

Personalization sometimes can be perceived from a simple comment. Have you ever heard someone say, "I can't believe that he would ever consider doing such a thing?" Or "How can she eat that food or wear that kind of clothing?" Or "My friend got her hair colored the same color as mine. I am unhappy about that." When someone becomes invested in these kinds of judgments of another person, they are unconsciously merging with the other person's experience – as though no individuality is permitted. The one personalizing takes on the other person's choice or action by judging it as though it belongs to them. They define the situation in a skewed manner and add imaginary details to it. It is an encroachment on the other person's personal space.

If you do this, you likely believe that it is justified; however, it is not. Your perceptions are based on judgment-filled beliefs. If someone else does something that you dislike, you can still approach it in a respectful manner. When appropriate, you can communicate with them, seek to understand the whole situation, accept, and respect the other person's individual process while letting go of the belief that they are doing something to you. It is also inappropriate for you to decide what the right choice should be for another person. Every person will process their experiences in a unique manner. Most often, the other person is innocently acting from their own history, conditioning, beliefs, likes, dislikes, and needs. Your responsibility is to be clear about what is true for you while being open to discover and understand more about the people around you or to simply create boundaries as needed.

The following example involves a husband and wife with a history of addiction challenges. The husband was focused on learning, growing, and recovering. The wife was in denial of the problems that were created by her attachment to drinking. Her behavior was often reactive, compulsive, and characterized by black and white thinking. The man had made some behavioral changes; however, he still struggled with lack of self-confidence and was dependent upon the approval of others. Because of that dependency, he often personalized his wife's choices and felt victimized by her lack of understanding and support, as well as by her personal insults. He was unable to maintain a stable sense of discernment between his own inner experience and his wife's projections.

Through personalization, he took on her beliefs, behaviors, and actions as his own responsibility. He turned them into his own personal struggle. They were her beliefs, *inside of her*, yet he believed that her behaviors could somehow decide something for him. Also, he believed that his personal growth could not continue in a consistent manner without his wife approaching life and participating in the *same* way that he did. His lifelong programming had taught him that he had to look for sameness in his relationships and outside circumstances so that he could be okay with himself.

After some time, through intermittent contemplation and seeking, he was able to take responsibility for his own independent personal process. Because of his individual growth, his wife could not relate to him in her usual manner. She felt rejected by him when he consciously chose in a purposeful way rather than engaging in their old habitual patterns. She believed that he was doing something to her. In those moments she would lash out, call him names, or make up lies about him. When she personalized in this way, he also sometimes personalized her while losing sight of his own path. They both merged with and took ownership of what the other person did or did not do, which led to back-and-forth fighting. In those moments, neither one of them could consciously maintain a focus or clear understanding of their own intentional, purposeful, rational inner experience. They had moved into a habitual reactive state of personalizing. Over a period of many years, they resolved this through individual self-inquiry. They created greater harmony between themselves.

In this next situation a woman named Anna habitually perceived the comments and actions of others to be about her. She could be at work, hear one person offer a compliment to someone else and feel slighted because they did not also compliment her. Then someone got a pay raise at work and even though Anna was very accomplished and made lots of money, she felt vindictive toward her co-worker. Her perception was that something unjust was being done to her when another person was compensated or acknowledged. She personalized it. In another situation while visiting a local bar, she was having a casual interaction with a stranger. A close friend of the stranger came into the bar. When this man bought his close friend a drink and did not also buy one for this woman, she became angry and felt as though he insulted her in some way. These were all situations with her personalizing the choices and experiences of other people. She was making it about her when it had nothing to do with her.

The next example involves a man named Bruce and a woman named Jill who lived together. Bruce did not know how to be fully present and directly process shared personal experiences with Jill. Because of this, he could not naturally navigate the unfolding emotions within himself or in other people.

The programming that he carried came about as a result of him going to boarding school when he was growing up. He was not allowed to process his needs or responses in an open context with others. Instead, he was taught that all feelings of conflict or spontaneous need had to be logically processed through the mind in a black and white manner and then put aside. Otherwise, he would be perceived to have done something wrong toward others. In his school, there was no deep human process for individual or shared discovery. Any authentic spontaneous expression of emotion was strongly discouraged. When someone was not able to control the outward display of an emotional need, they were reprimanded. Each boy was expected to always be in control of his emotions. Self-worth was reinforced in accordance with how well they followed the rules. To process on an authentic level was perceived to be bad and dangerous. To process through the structure of the mind was good and safe. Since this is what he learned, Bruce carried this approach into his adult relationships.

When it came to his partner Jill's emotional needs, Bruce believed that many of them were not valid. He believed that they were abnormal and needed to be put in the right place through a mental process. He continually tried to lead her away from direct feelings and into a state of black and white mental choices. He was unconsciously dominating her right to feel. Because she was unable to mirror what he had learned, he felt as though he was being wronged. He personalized it. It seemed illogical to him, that he should be expected to accept the opposite of what he had been taught.

Initially, Jill put a lot of effort into trying to help him to understand the reasons why she felt a certain way. She knew the difference between an emotional response and reaction. However, when she did have an appropriate emotional response, such as sadness, frustration, fear, or exuberant joy, he perceived all of it to be a reaction. None of her emotional responses were valid in his mind.

On occasion, when Jill went along with Bruce's expectations, she was enabling his behavior. This approach provided him with a false sense of safety and control. He expected her go along with his belief so that he could be comfortable. Because he perceived most of her emotions as reactive, he personalized her rather than trying to understand her. Eventually she became angry. He was not capable of understanding her. He was unable to consider what was outside of his programming, and she did not know how to create boundaries with his behavior.

As the stalemate continued, she felt controlled and dismissed by him. She responded more often with frustration and anger. Her emotions were no longer clean and authentic. She had moved into a state of constant struggle. She was personalizing him in response to him personalizing her.

Jill and Bruce both had the desire to share their perceptions and needs with one other and to be understood. Their intentions were the same; however, their understanding of how and to what degree that should or could be done were different. They did not realize that they had learned different ways to make sense of their inner experiences. This led to confusion, frustration, and blame; they both felt like victims. They each felt like the other was causing their suffering. What they needed was a process of curiosity and open-minded listening to access an understanding of their individual beliefs so that they could then see their options for change or to acceptance one another. If a process of curiosity and discovery completely disappear from a relationship, it can deteriorate into a hopeless, black and white, win-lose dynamic.

They both needed to reach a point where they were willing to let go of the struggle – the desire to force their own way onto the other person. Neither person had full conscious awareness of what was actually happening. Neither one of them had any conscious intent to harm the other. There were no victims. Therefore, there was no one to blame. Personalizing occurred from a lack of understanding and an unconscious desire for escape from the struggle. They needed to learn a process for distinguishing between fantasy and truth. As mentioned before, they also needed to be curious and apply good listening skills

Transitioning Beyond Your Conditioned Blueprint

to reach an overall understanding of one another and make new choices for change when possible.

In the following example you will see how it is also possible to personalize your own thoughts and actions in a self-bullying manner. Hypothetically, one day you decide to go visit an acquaintance named Amy. Based on the limited time you have spent with her, it seemed like good idea. However, as soon as you arrived at her house, she began to unload all of her problems onto you. She complained about most aspects of her life. You ended up feeling drained with a headache. It was an unpleasant experience. Instead of acknowledging what you learned and how you might create verbal boundaries in the future, you relentlessly blamed, judged, and criticized yourself while feeling like a victim of your own choice. Your internal dialogue included comments such as, "I should have known; why didn't I ask more people about her?" "What was I thinking?"

In this case, the statement, "I should have known," would be projecting the idea that you can know something before you participate in an experience. This is nothing more than a self-created, unreasonable story which contains unrealistic self-blame. In this hypothetical example, you would have been personalizing your own relationship with yourself. Instead of blaming yourself, it would have benefited you to bring your focus inward to witness, discern fantasy from truth, understand your own beliefs, seek to discover what you could learn, and apply it in future experiences. With this practice, you could discern what is possible or not, and create inner boundaries with your own thinking and reactions.

Another common practice of personalizing can occur when two people have a conversation and one person misinterprets a comment to mean something about them. For instance, Joe said to Mike, "My wife and I watched a great movie last night and ate two pizzas. It was nice." Mike responds with a defensive tone, "I can't eat that stuff! I'd get heavier than I already am." His comment makes it clear that he did not receive what was actually being shared with him. Joe shared something about himself and his wife, and then Mike made it about himself. Defensive or judgmental undertones will be present in this type of response.

In another example Sally and Martha were having a conversation about their evening routines. Sally described the happenings of her day and says, "Come eight o'clock, I'm just so tired that I have to get into my bed. I read for a little while, and then shut off the light and go to sleep." Martha says, "Well, I can't go to bed at eight o'clock. That is my most productive time of the day. I'd get way behind." She put herself in a defensive role, instead of responding to the details of what Sally shared with her. She was not listening to what Sally said. Instead, she was comparing herself to Sally and projecting the idea that Sally was making suggestions about her. This can lead to confusion and unnecessary tension.

In a family with a wife named Charlotte, husband Peter, and young daughter Amy, tensions existed because of a misconception on the mother's part. The daughter Amy, an only child, was innately more comfortable with boys and her father than with her mother or other females. The mother personalizes the situation. She imagined that a child should relate to both parents in the same manner. With Amy giving Peter more attention, Charlotte felt diminished, like a victim. Because Charlotte did not recognize or understand the uniqueness of each person, she presumed that her husband must have been doing something to make the child like him more. This led her to blaming both of them for the effects of what she created in her own mind. The accusations were mostly unspoken but could be perceived in her tone of voice, attitude, and body language. There was confusion and misinterpretation over the imaginary projections created by Charlotte's mind and the natural authentic behavior of the child. There was an inability to know how to discern truth from imagination. The mother's lack of understanding led to personalization and blame.

Part of the solution would be for Charlotte to become curious, ask open-ended questions, seek to understand her own beliefs and her daughter's while learning how to recognize the individuality of each person. In this way, Charlotte might be able to accept what she sees in her daughter as Amy's natural process along with an awareness that people are loved in different ways. This would eliminate the projection of stories, unreasonable expectations, confusion, and the alternating retaliatory or defensive behavior.

Next, we will look at a situation in a work environment. A woman Kristin worked for a design company in a managerial position. She had ten people under her and a boss who believed that she was doing a great job. The problem was between herself and the people that she supervised. One of her goals was to teach them how to function as a team. Kristin could see where the problems lay and came up with solutions; however, her delivery of this information come across as stern and angry. Most of the people in the team took this personally. They did not hear the message; they felt attacked and judged. Therefore, they became protective of themselves and resisted her suggestions. In response, she took their resistance personally. She felt that the problem was with them not liking her. The truth was that they didn't like her delivery.

When resistance goes up on either side, no one can freely perceive anyone else on a human or rational practical level. Kristin's boss was informed that Kristin came across as angry; however, Kristin defended it by insisting that she was only expressing passion and could not change because this was part of her nature. She commented that the team should be mature enough to look past her delivery to receive the information while learning what was necessary. She resisted an opportunity for understanding her co-workers and the conflict. Understanding is most often essential for harmonious resolution.

This scenario took place dozens of times while the shared turmoil escalated. An active curious state would have been useful for all parties. Kristin believed that her coworkers should have innately known how to look beyond their own emotional triggers to see the larger picture, but she could not consider that option for herself. She was unable to see a way to take responsibility for her own beliefs and choices.

The reactive behaviors of these people had been learned. Every situation provides an opportunity for people to learn more. However, if a person believes that their behavior defines them, then they will not see the way to change. In this case, fixed beliefs and resistance interfered with the learning process. Kristin needed to let go of her limiting beliefs, walk through her resistance, make a commitment to ongoing curiosity, inquiry, discovery, and contemplation while seeking to understand herself and others.

When new possibilities are discovered, they must be put to the test. When desired options don't work, then alternate choices will be available, and some of them will gracefully fit some of the time. Learning and change are inevitable. They are an innate part of life.

To take it a bit further, if Kristin wanted to create the opportunity for others to receive what she was offering, it would have been useful for her to show some interest in what her co-workers were capable of offering. Celebrating each person's small accomplishments would also be of significant value. Through curiosity she could present some purposeful ideas in an unattached manner while asking for input from others. She would have to start by perceiving each person on a human level rather than a piece of a problem. Each person's workplace value could be identified and validated. Kristin could become curious and ask questions to invite participation and discover new ideas.

It is important to acknowledge what others share so that they know that they have been heard. Curious questions are open ended; they are not leading or suggestive. If they are leading, then you have already included a suggestion of an answer in the question. If your idea or expectation has been interwoven into the question, then you have shut the door to discovery. When curiosity is interwoven into a question, it gives the message that you are receptive. Curiosity is most often perceived as a safe invitation for participation. An example follows.

I like some of what you have done with this design. However, based on the client's complaints, do you have some insights into a solution? Would you like to brainstorm with me or someone else? I am excited to see what comes of this! How much time do you feel that you need to create a new version of the design?

Even though the person in charge might think that they have all the answers, if they surrender some authority, they will be making room for a more creative, flexible team environment. There will also be room for others to bring fresh perspectives which may not have been available to the person in charge. At the same time, the manager or boss must still maintain a focused, anchored, confident, compassionate leadership position.

This next example concerns bullying. It involves a group of young girls in a chorus from a well-respected music school. They were very competitive and ranged in age from 10 to 14 years old. Most of the girls hoped to be chosen to perform a solo piece in each show. Veronica was the youngest and most talented of the group. Some of the older girls had been with the group for many years longer than she had but did not practice nearly as much. Veronica spent hours each day singing. The teacher was quite pleased with the broad range of Veronica's voice and consistently chose her to perform at least one solo for every performance. Three of the older girls did not like the praise and attention that she got. In their minds she was a problem. They felt that she was doing something to them simply by being present and sharing her natural abilities. They personalized her unique individuality. They tried to bring her down with snide remarks, eyerolls, and they ganged up on her as a threesome when the teacher was not looking. They were abusive; however, the teacher was afraid to say anything for fear of repercussions from parents who had proven to be difficult themselves. Several of the parents displayed the same behavior. The teacher previously had observed the father of another student stand up to one of these mothers only to have the whole thing turned around on him. The woman became dramatic while accusing him of being a bad person for confronting her. In this way she could avoid taking responsibility for her own and her daughter's behavior.

The girls often bullied Veronica to the point of tears; however, she still rose to the occasion and did the best that she could do during each class and performance. Because the three girls constantly compared themselves to her, they could not bear to look at her. They made themselves feel inferior by positioning Veronica as someone who was wronging them with her well-developed talent. They wanted her to go away. They were tormented by their own anger which was a result of their envy.

With her mother's validation, guidance, and coaxing, Veronica was eventually able to take a confident stand for herself. She realized that another person's words, perspective, or emotional reactions could not alter or diminish her individual identity. She took ownership of herself. When in their presence, she exuded a humble confidence. While looking straight at them, her response to the unkind statements was, "Why do you want to be so mean? Are you here to focus on me or your dance lesson?" Or she might say, "Why do you think that you are choosing to be so unkind? How does it make you feel when you do that?" Then she would look or walk away. She had compassion for them and the suffering that they imposed upon themselves. Through her courage to take a stand and create boundaries, she learned how to create a natural safe place for herself as well as build self-confidence.

The girls had personalized Veronica's talents. All three of them lacked confidence. They tried to get rid of their inadequacies by transferring them onto another person. By example, their parents had taught them to compare, be envious, personalize, dominate, and create drama. If they saw someone else display doubt, they could temporarily feel that it was outside of themselves – not inside. They subconsciously wanted others to feel shame so that they would be distracted from feeling their own guilt and shame. An ongoing state of powerlessness fueled the need for them to consistently have someone in their grasp and to victimize through their bullying behavior. They did not know that they were being tormented by their own programming and imaginations.

Do you recognize any similarities from any of these examples of personalizing that are taking place in your own experience? If so, write down the details.

Transitioning Beyond Your Conditioned Blueprint

Can you see how your own subconscious mind has been leading you to believe things about yourself and others that do not serve you? To create effective change, you will need to take responsibility for discerning truth from fantasy, realize that every person has their own beliefs and unique way of processing life, and acknowledge the boundaries needed for taking appropriate responsibility for yourself and others. You must also let go of any dependency on validation from others. When you accept the actual possibilities and limitations in any situation, then your options become clearer. To accomplish this, you need to practice witnessing your reactions and situations with curiosity, contemplate them, and know that another person's suggestions cannot decide things for you. Likewise, you cannot decide another person's identity, perceptions, intentions, process, etc. Seek to understand the similarities, but also the differences between yourself and others. In this way, you can make choices based on what is real with appropriate boundaries in place. Your own imagination and lack of understanding are the culprits when it comes to blurred boundaries between you and someone else. As you bring your focus inward now, can you take ownership in any of these areas where you have been projecting faulty beliefs, made-up stories, and dependency on someone else? Write down what you have discovered in detail.

As you can see, it is important to weigh the real facts of your situation, while also seeking to understand how you have been relating to other people. Now go deeper with your contemplation. Through honest, curious inquiry, can you identify the exact behaviors or faulty perspective that have been keeping you stuck? Also, look at alternate choices. Explain your discoveries in detail.

Transitioning Beyond Your Conditioned Blueprint

_____

You may find that when you acknowledge an alternate way of thinking and choosing, your ego wants to fight with you to maintain the familiar habits. Do you feel some internal stubbornness or resistance surfacing?

If so, write down the details.

___

When judgment or resistance is present, contemplate it rather than fighting with it or falling victim to it. It might feel like an impediment or a wall that is preventing you from taking the necessary steps to accomplish your goal. When you approach your resistance with curiosity, you will discover the faulty beliefs behind it. Once you understand that your avoidance is made up of judgment, fear, and a desire for something else, then you can transition through it. You must meet yourself and the moment as it is. Then you can proceed with any newly discovered choices. Accept that your situation is what it is and work with it from a basis of truth and real options. For change to happen, you must make new rational choices and participate with them. As you proceed through your experience, each choice acts as a step and leads to another choice in your process. Walk through and continue to challenge the tendency to personalize in all of its variations. This will naturally open up space. It will be beneficial for you to contemplate for the purpose of understanding the various layers of your experiences as they unfold. Once you gain an understanding, you will likely realize more choices. Proceed courageously.

Steps for transitioning beyond the habit of personalizing

1. Notice when you are blaming or judging someone else. Bring your focus inward to witness your thoughts and emotions while being curious. Through curiosity, seek to understand what is happening.
2. Notice the reasons why you are judging that person. Also, notice what your beliefs are about their role with you and your role with them. Do you feel a dependency for them to perceive you or respond to you in a certain way?
3. Notice if you are believing that someone else should know your feelings, thoughts, and needs without you having communicated any of that to them.
4. Now, make further inward inquiry into your reactions and beliefs to see what else they are indirectly suggesting.
5. Are you imagining that someone else is responsible for agreeing with you or responding to your unspoken beliefs, perspectives, or choices? Have you chosen to experience yourself in a diminished way because of the actions or inactions of another person?
6. Are you expecting someone to fulfill one of your personal needs? If you would like someone to share in a need, then ask them to do so. They may or may not oblige you. Accept the outcome. Sometimes, you will be the only one who can understand a particular need and respond to it. Once

you recognize that you are the one diminishing yourself while imagining that another person is doing it, then the truth can free you. You can choose to stop doing it to yourself.

7. Do you believe that another person can alter your personal experience with words or ideas? This is not possible. You only become diminished if you unconsciously decide to take on a diminished state. If a direct, indirect, or unconscious suggestion has been made, it is inside of the other person. It is not inside of you unless you choose to put it there. Shift your focus into something that is meaningful and true for you. Then own it. This brings you out of dependency.
8. Seek to recognize the difference between real facts and fantasy and untruths suggested by the use of words like should be, could be, if only, etc. They are not fact based. Sometimes it is necessary to accept the unexpected or unpleasant facts of reality when alternate options do not exist. Accepting does not mean that you agree with or condone a particular behavior or choice. It just simply means that you accept it as a fact.
9. Let go of any beliefs that keep you stuck such as those that involve competition, self-righteousness, envy, judgment, blame, or guilt. These are often present due to a lack of confidence. Increase your confidence through participation in real possibilities and create healthy boundaries. Be curious. Seek to discover, understand, and test the validity of your perspectives and beliefs through sharing and inquiry. Invite others to share so that you can experience and understand their unique individuality.
10. If you feel the need for more understanding from someone else, ask them if they are interested to know more about your thoughts and experience. If they are interested, share more details. In the end, they may or may not understand what you share. Seek to discover and understand their perspectives, beliefs, and intentions through non-suggestive questioning. Do not assume anything; otherwise, it is likely that you will make unclear decisions that are based on fantasy.

Transitioning Beyond Your Conditioned Blueprint

11. Identify any unspoken assumptions or suggestions behind your own thoughts and words. Be aware that when this occurs, you are processing or deciding things for someone else.
12. Notice when you may be deciding things based on imagination rather than the facts. Sometimes when a person witnesses something real or hears something true, they will immediately reject it while replacing it with something that was fabricated by their own mind. Be open to considering the individual experiences of others; however, use your discernment for identifying truth and falsehoods.
13. Alternate between witnessing the other person and yourself with an open mind. You could do this while the actual situation is taking place or as you recall it. Notice when you are interjecting stories or judgments into your interpretation of the experience. Make an effort to refrain from doing so. Instead ask questions for the purpose of accessing a greater understanding of an individual.
14. Accept the reality that you cannot know what is true without participating, and even then, nothing is concrete in a fixed way. Discovery is subjective and requires an ongoing process.
15. Seek to identify any resistance that you may have to the situation. Resistance is made up of fear, judgment, and a desire for another reality. This will take you out of the moment. It is not productive. It often comes from an unconscious desire to make things predictable. Recognize the resistance and walk through it with courage and curiosity.
16. Take note of when you are expecting yourself to be the same as another person or others the same as you. Sameness is a lazy person's approach. Differences are always there. You are not required to find a place of sameness within the differences. Know that others legitimately have their own experience, and you can respect them even when you don't agree. Also, each person has a right to their own process for discovery and learning. It is also natural for people to have different capabilities. Every human will have unique truths and challenges. Know that diversity in all things is the most predictable, natural expression of life.
17. Once you have more clarity about yourself, pay attention to the other person while holding the intention of seeing them as an individual and

understanding them as such. You are not meant to connect with everyone in the same way or to lose any part of yourself because someone else is different than you.
18. Make note of any adjustments needed for personal responsibility and stop taking inappropriate responsibility for others. Let go of any dependency for validation from another person. Confidence is developed primarily through honest participation – not validation from others. Seek to understand, not to control or possess.
19. You must seek to understand yourself and others from the basis of individuality rather than attempting to dominate, control, blame, or judge. Contemplate the value of any differences in each situation. Mutual understanding may or may not be possible. If it is not likely, then respect the outcome whether you are pleased or not.
20. Identify your own beliefs, responsibilities, needs, and goals with honesty; create boundaries where appropriate. Participate for discovery. In this way, you will develop personal trust, safety, confidence, and you will more often feel grateful. This approach will support you in your ever-changing experiences while bringing about your greatest potential to be present.

As you honestly challenge your own internal beliefs and patterns of reaction, you will be testing and discovering new ways of participation with yourself and the outer world. When you are present and discern truth, boundaries will naturally fall into place. The irrational needs to compete, defend, dominate, be submissive, or to create fantasy and drama will not be present in those moments. Remember, an ongoing commitment to practice brings about change.

-20-

What are personal boundaries?

The distinction between the identity of one person and another is one example of a boundary. A boundary crossing takes place when a person projects their own perspectives, preferences, judgments, choices, etc. onto another person with the expectation of them functioning accordingly. Boundary crossing also occurs when you make decisions for someone else, either in your mind or through direct interaction, instead of seeking to understand and accept the other person's individuality. Each person has their own process, perspectives, approaches, freedom of choice, etc. Without direct inquiry, you can know little about anyone else. Even when you do share or inquiry, you will still never completely know anyone, nor will they completely know you because who we are is mostly inside of us. Therefore, seek to offer understanding and access understanding. In this way you will be more likely to understand appropriate boundaries.

Simple examples of boundary crossing may include you giving unwanted advice based on your own preferences about how to think, make decisions, dress, speak, or eat. When this happens, you will have confused the lines of responsibility between yourself and the other person. You are not respecting the other person's right to choose for themselves or have an individual process. When taken to the extreme, this can foster a powerless state in that person or give you a false sense of superiority.

Inappropriate roles can also create boundary crossings and complicate relationships. A common example of this can occur between parents and children, for instance when children transition into adult roles. Sometimes the parent will continue to relate to their son or daughter as though they are still a child instead of moving into an adult relationship with appropriate boundaries. In this situation, the parent may tend to evaluate the son's or daughter's relationships or personal choices while giving unwanted opinions and advice. It is also possible that a parent may continue to provide for an adult son or daughter in the way that they would provide for a child. This behavior often reinforces a powerless state in the son or daughter.

Another example of overstepping is manipulation, when someone takes advantage of another's kindness through a sense of entitlement. You will see this in situations where envy is present, and a sense of entitlement takes hold. A manipulative person may also misrepresent themself as accomplished and seek to take credit for another person's efforts, knowledge, or accomplishments. The use of manipulation as a boundary crossing becomes obvious in the following example.

This example concerns a man who had a grandiose view of himself. He routinely placed great importance on the way that others perceived him in all areas of his life. This took all of his energy, distracted him from participating in a full range of possibilities and led to ongoing situations of self-sabotage. He took personal actions for fulfilling his goals on a surface level, but then all efforts would grind to a halt. He was unable to sustain the effort needed the meet the discomfort of unexpected challenges head on. This powerless state led him to depend upon others though a sense of entitlement with would flip-flop with envy. His handsome appearance and charisma were personal gifts that he learned to use for the purpose of gaining attention and getting what he needed on a practical level. The attention validated his never-ending desires and the belief that he could get whatever he wanted from almost anyone he encountered. However, it did not provide him with the confidence or skills he needed to proceed successfully in any aspect of his life.

When he presented his wants through masterful charm, confident entitlement, or suggestions of guilt toward others, most people could not recognize that he was making decisions for them through manipulation. They most often had no idea that he was crossing boundaries. Early on he developed a role of entitlement that led to some very effective manipulative patterns. When he did not have money to support himself, he knew how to twist another person's sense of responsibility to make them believe that he was a victim or that his situation was their fault, and they needed to address the problems for him. His display of charm and helplessness, along with projected blame and guilt were regular components of this. It was often based on the fact that they had money, and he did not. The financial worth that was produced through the efforts of other's was regularly high jacked. His emotional response to the people providing for his needs was a mix of temporary gratitude, satisfaction, envy, and resentment. Even though he constantly felt powerless, he never made an in-depth inquiry of the feeling. Therefore, no deep personal understanding was attained. He continued to overstep the boundaries of others through his false belief that they were responsible for his comfort and well-being. If other people did not pretend along with him, his response would often be one of venomous anger. The anger was used to dominate and control people. The goal was to make decisions for others so that he could benefit at will.

Transitioning Beyond Your Conditioned Blueprint

At times, when he witnessed others in need of money, it would remind him of his own inadequacies. This would drive him to acquire additional money from his enabling sources so that he could give it to the person in need and feel temporarily exulted. Boundaries were crossed as he unconsciously processed and took action for the other person. A sense of false confidence temporarily took place as he brought them to safety – something that he was unable to do for himself. He would feel offended and wronged if at any point the other person discovered and acknowledged the true source of the money.

His overstepping of boundaries was driven by his insecurities and lack of participatory experience. This behavior was exacerbated by his conditioned desire and expectation for others to take responsibility for him, to pretend, to accept his falsehoods, and to succumb to his manipulative strategies. He personalized the actions and inactions of others. Additionally, he could not perceive a process for building his own life because other people consistently enabled him, providing him with the rewards of their efforts. They did not perceive their own boundary crossing when they inappropriately took responsibility for his desires and rewarded him for his manipulation. His fragmented processing did not afford him a means of seeing the larger picture. He was not able to perceive the lack of value or behavioral inadequacies in his actions. This is typically realized through a clear discernment of truth vs. fantasy, contemplation of cause and effect, and the ability to accept personal responsibility. Discomforts or suffering did not lead to an adequate enough process for ongoing honest participation with life and the building of confidence, trust, and the courage to consistently challenge himself or to walk through personal fears and access the unknown. For this to take place, complete participation with goals and obstacles are necessary. Without this, a successful relationship with life is most often not realized.

In another boundary crossing example, a highly controlling, abusive woman named Rosetta was married to a man named Fred. From the beginning of the marriage Rosetta would get triggered if Fred did anything to give the appearance of being an individual separate from her. On rare occasions when he did function as an individual, she perceived him to be doing something to her. If he chose to watch a show about fishing or sports, she would yell at him while suggesting that he was watching garbage. In her mind the news was more important. She liked to have it on all day long. Fred was expected to do all of the cooking, yet Rosetta would decide what the menu would be. He could not make a suggestion about what type of food he would like to prepare without having her attack his decision as stupid. His activities away from the house were timed. He was not allowed to run late. If he did, she would interrogate him and threaten to burn his clothes. There was no distinction or space between the two of them. He was required to live as an extension of her. Individual boundaries did not exist.

He did not stop her from doing this. Instead, he felt powerless and depended upon his internalized scenarios of drama for a false sense of relief from the abuse. Only in his imagination did he take a stand or yell at her or tell her how he felt. He lived with internalized judgment and anger toward her. Occasionally, he would complain to an outsider while hoping to draw them in as an ally. However, his relief was short lived as he would go back home again. Because he did not take a firm stance and say NO to the abuse, he also suffered on another level as his own mind sought to address the problems internally while replaying the unresolved turmoil over and over on a daily basis. He was tormented. His lack of external boundaries led to an inability to create boundaries with the workings of his own mind. He would have likely needed to leave the situation for healing to take place.

The next example presents a father's impatience with his son. Clyde, the father, constantly imagined how his teenage son Gary should act. When Gary cut the grass at the family home, Clyde stood in the doorway telling him to go faster rather than allowing Gary to go at his own pace. The father was always in a hurry. When they had plans to go out and about anywhere, Clyde expected Gary to be ready to go at the same time as him. Gary also responded slowly in conversation. It was his way to respond thoughtfully. His father could not understand this. He saw it as problematic because Gary was different than him. Clyde constantly criticized Gary. Clyde could not perceive any individual process or approach beyond his own.

To have appropriate boundaries, Clyde would have to recognize that each person is different, and they should not be expected to process their experiences in the exact same way as another person. Also, Gary could respectfully acknowledge his father's perspectives while remaining in his own identity. For example, he could say, "I understand that you are comfortable doing things differently than me. I also have my own individual way of doing things that is unique to me. This way is natural for me, and I'm fine with it."

The next example concerns a woman who grew up with two self-centered parents. She was expected to automatically know what they wanted from moment to moment. Their needs were what mattered. Hers were seen as problematic. As a child she learned to put her own feeling, needs, perspectives, and preferences in the background while being hypervigilant to respond to theirs. This carried over into her adult life. If someone had a problem, she felt responsible for resolving it. She would project herself into the shared stories and experiences of others and process them in a personal manner while becoming attached to the outcome. She could not clearly discern appropriate responsibilities for herself or for other people. She also sought to please others, take action to avoid conflicts, and see that everyone's comforts were met to the detriment of her own well-being. She often felt exhausted, frustrated, and disappointed when others continued to have unresolved problems. Her investment in making things right for others distracted her from herself.

Can you recognize any area where you routinely cross boundaries with another person, or they cross boundaries with you? Write down the details.

_____
_____
_____
_____
_____
_____
_____
_____
_____
_____
_____
_____
_____
_____

Write down the ways that you will change your behavior to support healthy boundaries with yourself and others.

Transitioning Beyond Your Conditioned Blueprint

Steps for creating healthy boundaries

1. Observe your behavior to see where you may be projecting yourself into another person's experience. Perhaps you are deciding things for them, such as what their capabilities should be, a timeline for accomplishing something, what they should choose, how they should think, how they should proceed in a situation, how they should resolve something, etc.
2. If you notice yourself doing any of this, create some space within yourself through curiosity and witnessing. Then seek to understand rather than attempting to change, judge, or dominate the other person. Ask direct questions that will help you to make discoveries and to gain understanding. You might ask yourself questions such as, "Am I expecting someone else to function or process in the same way that I do? Am I able to perceive the other person and myself as unique individual people? Am I imagining what the other person's intentions might be instead of asking them? Do I have resistance to discovering the other person's individual

process? Am I willing to let go of the tendency to project decisions through judgments or assumptions about the other person?
3. Now observe whether others are deciding in similar ways for you.
4. If you notice this happening, acknowledge their comments as an offering which you have the option to accept or not. If they are not useful, you could say something like, "Thank you for sharing your ideas or your personal approach about what I am doing. I understand you more now. This is my approach based on my present capabilities. I am comfortable with that." You could also say, "Have you noticed that this approach is natural for me, and it works? It is nice that you have also found an approach that works for you."
5. It is important to discern individual responsibility and to make appropriate choices to support that. For instance, if someone is trying to manipulate you through guilt, you might say to them, "I can see that you are uncomfortable in your current situation and would like me to resolve that or do things that will make you feel better. However, I do not see that to be appropriate for me or you. I wish you the best in figuring that out." Alternatively, perhaps you decide that it is appropriate to help them discover new choices. In that case you might say, "If you would like to brainstorm some possible actions for a solution, I can help you to do that. However, I cannot resolve your situation for you."

-21-

What is drama and how does it get created?

Drama takes place when pieces of reality are taken out of context and intertwined with fantasy to create the illusion of control and cover up a person's fears. The offender likely is not fully conscious of what they are doing or why they are doing it. Drama serves to pacify unconscious fears about direct participation and the negotiation of real options in life. It also distracts people from taking personal responsibility for recognizing, understanding, or accepting the diversity of individual experience or discovering the real facts of a situation. When a situation appears threatening to a person, they reenact their personal struggle outside of the circumstances where it occurred with others who were not involved. In the moment, the person will often push their own needs, perspectives, or ideas aside and then, blame others for *wronging* them after the fact. They deny themselves and others the opportunity to access understanding through honest, direct participation. When this takes place, no new discoveries can occur. Generally, a defensive blame-based story is added to a personalized piece of the experience. When a trigger producing situation first occurs, the person will often pretend that they are just fine – they say nothing. They exit the original situation and formulate a story around the piece of conflict or the person that triggered them. They are likely to profile the subject from a basis of their own distorted view of the situation. In effect, they will create an imaginary puppet version of the person which can be directed through various made-up scenarios. They become falsely empowered in their role as a puppeteer. This occurs in their mind, but they do not recognize it. Self-imposed stress or even trauma will inevitably occur. However, this will not be recognized as self-created either. Blame will be projected at the real version of the person. The attacks often occur in a manner that is unbeknownst to the other person. The one who is being blamed often has no idea that the one blaming them has a distorted processing approach. They will end up confused by the misinformation. Since the perpetrator most often avoids direct participation, resolution is unlikely.

Sometimes the drama plays out directly in the situation where it got triggered for the purpose of manipulation. In this case, the person will reject reality when it does not fit their agenda. They present their desires in a magnified distorted manner and communicate through suggestions of guilt and blame toward others in an attempt to force compliance. If the guilt and blame do not work, then the person will often resort to anger to dominate the *will* of others.

Drama is very black and white. No contemplation, direct participation, or negotiations take place to discover or consider the individual experience of the other people, available choices, individual responsibility, or the difference between fantasy and reality. The person creating it most often fears the experience of direct participation, inquiry, discovery, consideration of real facts, and new choices. They may also have a fear of being wrong, a fear of conflict, of personal responsibility, and have an attachment to the imagined predictability of fantasy. Also, the person most often does not have the comprehensive skills to process their experiences effectively and directly. Fantasy and attachment to a desired imaginary outcome provide the fuel that keeps drama going. Pieces of truth will exist within drama; however, they will be tainted with many false ideas. The fantasy will turn any experience into a distorted version of the original experience. People often create drama to unconsciously control an imaginary replay of the original experience. You can learn to recognize various degrees of drama as active components of learned behaviors such as personalizing, judging, stubbornness, competitiveness, self-righteousness, envy, and manipulation.

Participation in drama is compulsive by nature. It is dependent upon fragmented perceptions and actions that must be endlessly carried out. The reward comes through the short-lived effects of dopamine release and the illusion of control. Drama is not reality based; therefore, it cannot support purposeful experience and value in life.

With patterns of drama, each person's sense of value and identity are based on the ideas from personalized judgments, perpetual use of labels, or fragmented concepts. They are disconnected from the overall truth of the experience where the conflict originated. There are ongoing attempts to resuscitate a fragmented past, manipulate the present, or step into a fictional future while interacting with imagined scenarios through fixed ideas and stories. This will cycle in a predictable fashion unless a person becomes consciously curious, chooses to discern fact from fantasy, participates to discover and understand the truth of their individual and shared experience. If a self-aware, truth-based person is drawn into the conflict, others are likely to aggressively attack them if they speak the truth. It is important to understand what is happening in this type of scenario.

When people have been indoctrinated into the unconsciousness of drama, their ego does not like to have the conditioned state interrupted. They will feel threatened by authentic experience or the truth of the moment. Their ego cannot perceive the wholeness of in-the-moment experience but takes comfort from the familiar fantasy patterns. When this has been their ongoing history, individuals will have little to no processing capabilities for accessing, comprehending, participating in, or integrating ongoing deep diverse wisdom and the larger truth of each experience. They will tend to evaluate the unfolding variables of each situation from a place of judgment while creating assumptions and projections. They will be unfamiliar with a curious, conscious approach. While trying to

Transitioning Beyond Your Conditioned Blueprint

preserve their own approach, they may refer to the one who is authentic as a liar, stupid, evil, or a troublemaker. They may try to invalidate any skills or abilities of the other person by referring to them as a phony or an imposter. They will unconsciously create and maintain a skewed version of the person that they can control on an imaginary level. The one who is under attack must not create a role of defense or defeat in response to the attacks. If this occurs, they will be held captive by the same paradigm. They must instead stay curious, seek to understand the capabilities and limitations of the other's behaviors, let go of any attachment to blame, create appropriate boundaries for health and well-being, and own their individual truths as well as their own ability to be present.

Keep in mind that there is no healthy role or way to participate in drama. Once you are able to understand drama and know when it is happening, you can challenge it by separating fantasy from fact and creating boundaries. In this way, you will transcend the likelihood of getting pulled into it. I will give you an example of how drama may occur in the following examples.

This case involved a woman who created an internal drama that was fueled by a fear of the unknown. She worked at a restaurant as a waitress. An opportunity had come about for her to go on an all-expense paid trip to Disney in Florida; however, she would need to ask for time off from her boss. The boss could be unsympathetic and demanding. She automatically fantasized a scenario about what would happen when asking for the time off. She imagined that her boss would not hear her or consider her needs. In response to the self-created fantasy, she developed a desire to go on vacation without having to seek his approval. From there, she added a trail of stories that further fueled her desire for an escape. She imagined that when asking for time off, the boss would get angry and tell her that she couldn't go. Then, in response to these ideas, she imagined telling him off, quitting her job, and alternated between the scenarios of getting a better job and her boss feeling guilty about it. This led to her feeling very judgmental toward him as well as more fearful of him.

As you can see, she created many details of a fantasy which evolved into stories which created internal stress and weakened her sense of confidence. She felt beaten up and traumatized. Meanwhile, she had no clear understanding that she had been interacting with fantasy figures of her own creation. In the end, she decided not to ask her boss for time off; instead, she secretly took her trip after calling in sick and claiming to have the flu. The healthy, rational approach would have been to simply explain the situation, ask for time off, and then make the next best choice based on the discoveries that came from a direct interaction with her employer. The stories that she told herself turned into a one-person theatrical performance. Later, the guilt that got created from lying caused worry and made it difficult for her to enjoy her vacation. She feared that her boss would find out and fire her. Her resistance to directly participate led to the creation of stories about her boss and work situation which led to lots of internal drama, her own suffering, compromised her ability to discover truth, and diminished her happiness.

The next example involved a breakdown of any possibility for healthy connection in a family whose members did not learn to process their experiences in a direct manner. Roles of dominance and submission prevailed, along with a win/lose approach to conflict. These behaviors were intergenerational. When a disagreement took place within the family, it was not confronted in the situation where it was created. It was not talked about directly with the person with whom purposeful discussion, discovery, and negotiation was needed. Many harmful stories were created that contained distortions, blame, judgment, passive bullying, and fostered ill-will toward the person who was being attacked. Once the role of villain was transferred onto the person who was being scapegoated, an unconscious decision was made to reject them totally – their whole being was rejected as bad. They were temporarily or permanently shunned from the family as other kin were drawn in as allies. The individuals who decided to participate in the fantasy were attached to winning at all costs. There was no ability to comprehend, understand, or respect individual perspectives, needs, or differences. There was no understanding, love, or compassion – only judgment, dominance, or compliance. As new challenges arose, the assigned role of scapegoat would sometimes shift from one person to another. Each time, the orchestrator of the drama was the leader and the bully. Yet while family members were in the immediate vicinity of the supposed enemy, they pretended that nothing was going on even though everyone could feel an undercurrent of passive bullying, judgment, and condemnation toward the target. The one who was under attack felt trapped, but also pretended that nothing unusual was occurring. However, after the fact, this person was able to acknowledge what had happened and responded with internalized, cyclical thoughts of judgment toward the attackers. This was their only known defense. Family members didn't know how to see the humanity in one another. They didn't know that their individual differences were natural and created an opportune gift for discovery and learning. Curiosity invites an opportunity for understanding; this was foreign to them. The need for sameness, along with judgment to maintain control, kept everyone trapped in a state of struggle. No one was safe in that environment.

The next example involved a feud between three individuals. Feuds often begin with simple arguments or misunderstandings that become fueled by drama.

This situation involved a married couple and the married man's best friend. They were all in their twenties, just starting out in life, and had known one another since childhood. The couple announced to their friend that they were buying their first house. Feeling happy for them, the best friend congratulated them. The couple did not think that their friend was really happy for them because he did not express exuberant joy. They began to dramatize their faulty perspectives of him with other people. As others fed into the drama, it grew. Before long, they had created stories that depicted the best friend as an unkind and envious person. They developed an imaginary version of him that worsened by the day. They bounced it back and forth between themselves while creating pretend scenarios with it. Because they both had a historical addiction to drama, they could not recognize what was happening. Together the couple had created something that was completely untrue but treated it as though it was a fact of reality. After months of engaging with the imaginary character of their friend, they began to resist any direct contact with the person who had been their real friend. The couple, along with some other friends and family, had all to some degree been indoctrinated into falsehoods through repetitive participation with the imaginary scenarios involving the childhood friend. At that point, any encounter with the real person posed a threat. The couple feared that something in their behavior might be exposed as wrong, so contact was avoided at all costs. The couple sought to protect the fantasy while continuing to depict the man as the enemy with other people. The previous best friend made repeated attempts to challenge the stories but was met with hostility from the man and woman. He was shunned from their lives. The couple ended up as captives of their own self-created drama. Because they remained attached to what they had created, the truth was unavailable to them.

The previous example may seem extreme; however, it happens all too often. Feuds often begin with simple misunderstandings fueled by drama. People make assumptions, project imagined ideas, or create entire stories so that they can feel that their agenda is being supported while never putting the effort in to discover what is real. They accept the ideas that are fed to them by their conditioned mind. The only value in this is to learn from it; otherwise, it creates loss and suffering for everyone.

Another form of drama occurs when people fixate on one small detail of another's behavior – making a mountain out of a molehill. In this example, a woman Rachael was at a party with a friend who proceeded to speak in a loud voice. As she listened to her friend Ellen, she only heard the volume of her voice; she did not hear the message. She personalized it, judged it, and took it on as a personal problem. She proceeded to create a story in her head. Rachael imagined that other people would judge her for being with someone who spoke in a loud voice. She imagined her friend Ellen to be seeking attention, to be consciously inconsiderate, and wanting to embarrass her. She felt like something was being done to her and based Ellen's identity primarily on the one detail. Both personalizing and drama were involved here.

In this next example, a father by the name of Tim shared the same story with his friend Steven each time he visited. He engaged in the same conversation about his 30-year-old son. He grumbled about his son's intermittent employment. "Between jobs, he often has no money and expects to get some loot from me or someone else. He does not pick up after himself and has no passion toward life. He functions through patterns of envy and entitlement." Tim had a hard time embracing his own needs and setting boundaries when in the presence of his son. He complained to Steven about what a pain in the ass his son was – how he did not care about anyone. "He thinks that everyone else should deal with his discomforts, struggles, and make his life feel good for him. He is lazy; he expects whatever he needs to come from other people; he probably plans on living with me until the day I die – can't he see that I need my own space? He is probably laughing at me with his friends. He had better smarten up." Tim had forgotten how to perceive his son from a level of humanness. He felt powerless. He did not know how to create boundaries and say *no*. Because of this, he ended up feeling angry even though he was the one who allowed it to keep happening.

Tim perceived his son's identity primarily through the struggles that persisted between them. He felt trapped because he could not say no; therefore, no healthy boundaries existed. To escape the turmoil from the situation, Tim compulsively created scenarios of internal drama that he unconsciously drew others into. This only provided temporary relief. The same thing was allowed day in and day out. Instead of taking a stand for himself with choices that would stop the cycle, he was waiting for his son to make choices to remedy the situation. The necessary choices are often very different from the choices that a person desires. So instead of making some uncomfortable choices, Tim continued enabling and blaming.

His friend Steven had made repeated suggestions to him that perhaps he should learn to say no sometimes, give his son an ultimatum, and spend some quality time with him instead of perceiving him as a bad, broken person. Tim did not make use of the suggestions. He was afraid to change his own behavior, courageously take a stand, or make choices to support his own needs. He did not realize that a different approach could possibly bring different results. He was afraid of conflict – afraid of losing his son. Instead, he sought a false sense of temporary relief with the situation by airing his reactions verbally, creating distortions, and magnifying the unpleasant details repeatedly. The solution for Tim would have been to use curiosity and inquiry for the purpose of understanding his son, to share his own honest feelings without blame, to seek new possibilities while testing them one at a time, and to say NO to the things that clearly did not work for him.

As you can see, a participatory process between an idea and exploration, discovery, understanding, and change is missing when drama is present. The ability to approach a problematic situation with curiosity is lacking. There is a propensity to function with black and white perspectives, thereby creating struggles with subservient or dictatorial roles. With drama, a dominant position in a relationship will be desirable and translate into the feeling of being right and winning. In worse case scenarios, this type of patterning will make individuals susceptible to ongoing abusive relationships, create a sense of powerlessness or authoritarianism, and influence a victim mode or an addiction to controlling others. As a result of the suffering and desire to be free, it often leads to additional layers of compulsive behavior.

Can you recognize any situations of drama that have been or are now taking place in your life? Write them down here.

_____
_____
_____
_____
_____
_____
_____
_____
_____
_____
_____
_____
_____
_____
_____
_____
_____
_____
_____
_____
_____
_____
_____
_____
_____
_____
_____
_____
_____
_____

Transitioning Beyond Your Conditioned Blueprint

The negative effects of drama

1. Through your attachment to a belief that someone else should do or be a certain way, you are creating a dependency. This is part of drama.
2. Where curiosity is lacking, a discovery process is also lacking. This will leave you with set beliefs or stuck in a self-created fantasy that will keep you trapped.
3. You will be led by illusions that are fueled by fears, projections, and desires.
4. The fantasy element of it will limit the possibility of honest participation with other people or situations, thereby blocking your perception of rational choices, discoveries, purposeful sharing, and a sense of equality with others.
5. During times of conflict or anticipated conflict, there is a likelihood that you will fear the possibility of being judged and dominated by others. This

could lead you into reactiveness, defensiveness, and judgment toward other people as your imagination retaliates. You may fear the idea of being seen as wrong and defend your position at all costs. If this occurs, you will have a battle going on inside of yourself.

6. The fear of being seen as wrong can lead a person to function in a state of secrecy or denial.
7. The multi-leveled dysfunction of drama prevents people from accessing clear discernment and discovery within the larger overall experience of themselves, others, and any situation.
8. Drama fuels self-doubt and brings about self-sabotage.
9. You will be more prone to abusive relationships, and you will flip-flop between the roles of victim and bully.
10. You will trust fantastical ideas more than direct honest participation and discovery.
11. You will not know personal trust or how to have healthy boundaries with others.
12. Drama blocks an awareness of individuality, diversity, or unique experience from within each person and situation.
13. You will be unable to perceive the purpose and value of individuality and diversity. It will also be difficult to effectively navigate the ongoing, ever-changing details of interpersonal experiences.
14. The unsafe internal environment can create habitual negative projections or even paranoia.

In what ways are you personally compromised by drama? How does it affect the way that you relate to others?

_____
_____
_____
_____
_____
_____
_____
_____

Transitioning Beyond Your Conditioned Blueprint

When you learn to recognize drama and step into a direct experience of honest participation with yourself and others, you will be living in the direct unfolding of life while accessing purpose, values, the creation of healthy boundaries, the building of personal trust, and confidence. Along with this comes understanding, respect, acceptance, and compassion for self and others.

Explain any newly gained clarity. What do you plan to change in your behavior so that you can participate directly and honestly with yourself and others?

Transitioning Beyond Your Conditioned Blueprint

_____
_____
_____
_____
_____
_____
_____
_____
_____
_____
_____
_____
_____

A process for overcoming patterns of drama

1. First, you must recognize when you are engaged in a drama. If you are immersed in a judgmental, blame-based, repetitive struggle involving a situation, and/or yourself and another person, you are likely playing out a drama. Witness your thoughts. Are you judging yourself or someone else while projecting the ideas of could be, should be, or why not with stories created to support those assumptions?
2. Also notice any desire you have to reenact your story with someone outside of the original situation.
3. Next, you must witness and contemplate to discern the difference between fantasy and the truth-based facts of the experience. The truth is made up of the actual details that took place. These do not include assumptions or projected ideas. If it is true, nothing from your imagination has been added.
4. Are you adding blame in response to an unexpected outcome or an assumption that got created in your own mind? Take a step back and witness for the discernment of fact and fantasy.
5. Are you judging someone for thinking, feeling, perceiving differently than you or for having their own process, individual needs, or goals? As you

contemplate for discernment of truth, you may experience some resistance.

6. If you recognize some resistance, observe it, and seek to understand the beliefs behind it. Remember that resistance is made up of judgment, a desire for what is familiar, and an effort to reject what is new or different. Do not fight with it, but instead maintain a curious focus with it. Ask yourself questions about it. Patiently sit with each question and see what comes. You may experience more space or gain some insight. Resistance is a reaction and reactions are doorways into your subconscious, so do not be afraid of them. Judgment, personalization, blame, and impatience are also reactions.

7. When you follow the reaction inside of yourself, you will often access understanding and wisdom. So put your focus directly in the reaction while patiently allowing it to reveal faulty beliefs, set ideas, and hidden truths. Instead of trying to do anything to the reaction, give it the space to unfold on its own. This is how it becomes unraveled and cleared away. As you discover the truth, the reaction loses its power. You will then be left with some degree of understanding. You can witness and contemplate anything that surfaces from within the resistance or within a reaction.

8. Do not let your focus go outward when a reaction appears. If it does, it will likely become attached to the idea of someone or something for the purpose of creating a distraction from the turmoil or beliefs that triggered it. Outward attachment most often leads to judgment or blame toward yourself or other people. Some possible experiences that may arise from within the reactions could include fear, self-doubt, resentment, a belief that you do not have a right to stand in your truth, a need to compete with others for superiority, a faulty belief of compliance, an attachment to deciding and processing someone else's reality, the need to dominate and control situations or other people, etc.

9. Once you discern fact from fantasy, you can contemplate further. When you realize a limiting belief, fear, or judgment, contemplate those too. Then set the intention to walk through it while participating in a state of curiosity, so that you can discover something more. Part of the goal is to

replace judgment, blame, or defensiveness with open ended curiosity for the purpose of discovery and understanding within yourself.
10. Next, if possible, participate in an open-minded manner with other people for the purpose of discovery. Offer information that could provide an understanding of your personal experience and ask curious open-ended questions so that you can understand the other person better. You will not be inquiring or sharing to defend, prove, compete, satisfy a judgment, dominate, or seek approval. Through curious inquiry, you will be inviting the other person to share things with you that you may not know, so that you can gain a greater understanding of them. This also has the potential to inspire them to ask questions.
11. If you feel a desire to replay the initial experience with someone else, witness that desire with curiosity. Inquire into your motivations for doing it. Challenge yourself to refrain from acting on it unless it is to seek clarity about yourself and your own behavior. In some situations, you may need to engage with a therapist to accomplish this. Once you gain some clarity, this could be a new starting point for purposeful participation.
12. As you develop some ability to recognize drama, you will still have to apply your effort to discern fantasy from truth and redirect your focus until the new approach feels completely natural. Do not expect this process to happen all at once. At times, you will have to walk through fears and engage your courage.
13. Learning requires practice. Sometimes you will not see the progress; however, trust that it is happening. An ongoing commitment that is free of a timeframe will bring results.
14. As you learn how to directly participate in your life, you will become more deeply fulfilled while gaining trust in yourself, confidence, and greater understanding of yourself and others.

Chapter Seven

Confidence Matters

-22-

What is personal confidence?

When you are confident, you will not be looking for someone else to approve, agree with, or decide the value of your feelings, needs, choices, perspectives, or processes. You will be anchored in your own unique individuality. You will be embracing the process of personal growth with ongoing curiosity, discovery, contemplation, and participation. You will be testing new choices and integrating newfound wisdom. If you look to others to do your problem solving, decide the value of your abilities, or substantiate your level of knowledge, then you will not be present to discern truth from fantasy and to identify meaning, purpose, and value for yourself. You will be waiting for other people to decide things about you according to their own beliefs and personal conditioning. You will be giving someone else permission to decide your right to either struggle with or embrace your own experience. Remember a person's life history includes gathered wisdom and understanding, but also struggles, challenges, aversions, and behavior patterns which are unique to that person's life. It is their blueprint for them to live and work with – not yours. If you are dependent on others in this way, it will put you into a disempowered place. If you practice this self-sabotaging behavior, your position will be inferior to others – not equal. Equality takes place when you authentically participate, honor your uniqueness, discoveries, choices, create appropriate boundaries, and participate fully, thereby accessing a deep knowing. This is something that cannot be given to you by someone else. It is experiential. Therefore, an experience of it cannot be transferred from one person to another. A dependency-based type of false confidence sometimes takes place through over-identification with people with high social standing or through family hierarchies. This can also take place through association with the ideas of status from professional labels and educational degrees.

The following example depicts a life-long college student named George. He was 50 years old and had moved in and out of his parent's house multiple times, insisting each time that they were responsible for his fecklessness. They repeatedly fell prey to his accusations which were infused with suggestions of guilt. They paid for his living expenses, education, auto repairs, gym fees, phone bills, and entertainment expenses. Each time he moved back with his parents, he promised that he would do what was necessary to progress as an independent individual in the world. He earned more degrees and boasted about them with other people while looking for their praise. Many of the people around him saw through this; however, he did not. He gathered enough external trappings to give the appearance of financial success. He took whatever accolades he could get, which gave him a temporary lift similar to taking a drug. When an *important* person offered praise, it reinforced his patterned approach to life. He saw himself as living on the same level of success as them. He became angry when others did not give him this temporary boost. He was so accustomed and addicted to instant gratification from outside validation that a lot of his energy went into seeking it. He was not capable of meeting the diverse challenges of life to discover how to take charge of his own life. What he did not realize was that he had already learned a mini version of the process needed for success from applying himself in the educational system. He had a framework in place that he could apply to the broader experience of life.

Sometimes a person becomes confident in one area of life but feels inadequate outside of that area. For example, a person who feels confident while applying their skills and abilities through a role, such as work or a creative endeavor, may not be able to access a sense of personal trust and confidence outside of that role. If something does not feel predictable or familiar, the ego often struggles with a need to know beforehand. This takes a person out of the present moment.

Transitioning Beyond Your Conditioned Blueprint

If this unconscious fragmented approach goes on at length, a person may develop a habitual anxiety response when the necessity arises to participate on levels beyond what is familiar to them. For instance, they may be awkward on a social level when most of their focus has been on family, a creative endeavor, or a job.

An example of this takes place with Ron, a 45-year-old artist who had a passion for painting beautiful landscapes. The finished paintings were displayed throughout his house. On occasion, he invited friends for potluck dinners with the secret hope that they would engage with him through admiration of his artwork. For him, the art represented the parts of himself that he liked. He felt awkward when people showed an interest in other areas of his life. He only felt confident and capable when they engaged with him through conversations about what he created. When people came to visit and did not notice his artwork, he felt rejected. He personalized the experience and might comment, "I don't know why they bothered to come! They did not say anything about my paintings. I think that is so inconsiderate."

He not only had a fragmented, limited sense of confidence, he also personalized the situation while creating drama for himself. He was not able to trust in the value of his spontaneous individuality or overall uniqueness as a person. While in the presence of others, he functioned in a state of dependency.

Can you identify any areas of your life where a state of dependency exists in relation to your confidence?

_____
_____
_____
_____
_____
_____
_____
_____
_____
_____
_____
_____

Now, can you identify areas of confidence that come naturally for you as a result of well-developed experience, skills, or innate abilities? Notice how you are able to be comfortably present in those areas. Write down your examples and describe the differences between these and the examples of dependent confidence.

Transitioning Beyond Your Conditioned Blueprint

_____
_____
_____
_____
_____
_____
_____
_____
_____
_____
_____
_____
_____
_____
_____
_____
_____
_____
_____
_____
_____
_____

As you get a sense of what this feels like, it will be possible for you to transfer the essence of the natural confidence into other areas where you presently feel a lack of confidence. It will take practice, and you will make many discoveries. When functioning in a process of discovery, each new step that you take becomes a piece of your foundation of confidence and safety. You will need to embrace it by consciously acknowledging that you are the one participating with the skill, knowledge, experience, etc. Hence, confidence is built one step at a time through full conscious participation.

-23-
How does a person build confidence?

The more that you honestly participate in life, the greater your confidence will be. Through being curious, engaging, discovering, discerning, surrendering, accepting, creating boundaries, and taking action you can come to trust your ability to respond to known and unknown situations. Sometimes you will need to apply your courage. To be truly confident, you must meet yourself where you are in any given situation, be open to learning more, and accept your natural limits. You must maintain an awareness of what you know while recognizing that what you know can be limited by your past experience, beliefs, and triggers. When you stay curious, there is an open door that leads to whatever comes next – to realizing and learning more. It may be new and different or a variation of what previously took place. The nature of life is change; it never repeats itself in the same way twice. This means that life is never really predictable or without struggles and discoveries. When you are confident, you will move with the struggles and discomforts more gracefully.

You must humbly recognize and celebrate your strengths, skills, abilities, accomplishments, and goals without the need to boast or prove yourself. It is important to embrace the experience of not knowing, looking awkward sometimes, needing help, and often proceeding without a clear understanding of a particular situation. The ability to surrender is important. This means that you will have to be committed to the practice of curiosity and be flexible with your goals. Know that there are no set rules that you must figure out or follow. Simply be honest, follow your values, and use discernment. As you participate in many different areas of life, you will be testing the possibilities within yourself and your circumstances to determine what fits or does not fit. As you learn how to choose in a clear and decisive manner, you will be learning boundaries. Appropriate boundaries with awareness of appropriate responsibilities between yourself and others will be recognized. You must participate with many layers of personal interest and needs, along with intervals of space and reflection to gain understanding and make purposeful choices. Confidence and personal trust are built through full participation and by taking one step at a time – these abilities do not instantly appear. They must be consistently practiced. Your experience will be varied as you participate in different types of situations such as personal interests, practical responsibilities, and the process for short-term and long-term goals. Contemplation will be necessary.

Contemplate your needs while looking at all areas of your life such as the social, professional, spiritual, creative, adventurous, intimate, health and fitness, etc. When you consciously participate on multiple levels of self, along with contemplation and actions for testing new choices, you will be building personal awareness and a deeper experience within all aspects of life. Where there is a lack of confidence, you probably have not consciously participated enough on that level with curiosity and a readiness to meet the moment in an exploratory manner. Whenever you don't know something, the not knowing provides a window for learning and taking in more variations of life.

Write down the specific areas where you are already participating as well as some areas where you would like to further engage so that you can build more confidence.

_____
_____
_____
_____
_____
_____
_____
_____
_____
_____
_____
_____
_____
_____
_____
_____
_____
_____
_____
_____
_____

_____
_____
_____
_____
_____
_____
_____
_____
_____
_____
_____
_____
_____
_____
_____
_____

Now, contemplate to see if you can recognize any obstacles that have gotten in the way of your participation, learning, growth, and the development of greater confidence. Write down your discoveries.

_____
_____
_____
_____
_____
_____
_____
_____
_____
_____
_____
_____
_____
_____
_____
_____
_____

Transitioning Beyond Your Conditioned Blueprint

Next, formulate a plan for greater participation in the areas where you lack confidence. You may need to engage your warrior mode to walk through any resistance or obstacles. Write down some of your thoughts and ideas in detail.

_____
_____
_____
_____
_____
_____
_____
_____
_____
_____
_____
_____

-24-

What are some of the challenges that you may encounter while building confidence?

The most common challenge in your process for discovery and change will likely be resistance. Resistance may contain fear, judgment, complacency, or a desire to keep or instantly get rid of a situation. Sometimes the psyche will prefer to remain in familiar comfortable circumstances. Attachment to habitual roles can get in the way of taking action and of personal growth. When this happens, a person will procrastinate, get distracted, and lose motivation. The cascading effects of this can sometimes lead to a fear of being judged, to self-judgment, to projections of failure, or to feelings of helplessness. When you feel stuck or overly attached, remember to contemplate your feelings as they arise. In this way you will gain some clarity and free yourself through greater understanding. However, you must remember that whatever you realize may need to be put into action. It is possible that a person will feel layers of resistance in between the various realizations. Learning and confidence building are not linear, so accept the unexpected.

Sometimes a person may have trouble transitioning from an idea into a participatory process that involves *many* steps. They may have some great ideas but are not able to put them into action. They feel motivation and fulfillment from the initial idea; however, when they think about making it happen their motivation goes away. This often happens because a person is unfamiliar with the difference between the idea of something and a process for bringing it into reality.

To begin, you need only be aware of the first step. Once you take the first step, then you will see the next appropriate step. Sometimes you may have to access more information by researching the internet, inquiring with other people, contemplating, or giving space to the situation. Do not expect to know the entire process or outcome before you take many steps. Just take whatever step is available and remain open and curious to discover more. Life happens one step at a time. Getting stuck often occurs when the ego is resistant to the process of surrender and an openness to receive from the unknown.

Every time you take a step, you will be entering a new and unfamiliar experience. What you intended may or may not take place. However, the ego desires predictability, a specific timeframe, or instant change. None of this is possible in exactly the way you imagine it to be. The mind cannot predict authentic process. This is revealed as experience unfolds. You must realize that you cannot jump into a ready-made new place that matches your idea. Realistically, as you proceed with each step, you will make discoveries, negotiate options, build new skills, access various levels of personal awareness, and discover the need for more inquiry or the need to create boundaries. Your participation supports a continuous unfolding process. As you proceed, you will need to alternate between states of curiosity, receptivity, contemplation, surrender, acceptance, stillness, and participation. The value of each step must be experientially acknowledged so that the wisdom of it is integrated into your subconscious mind. You will find that there is value in both pleasant and unpleasant experiences. As you consciously honor the value of each step, you will be anchoring it. The benefit of possible learning will always be present in the process and outcome of each choice. Embrace this, receive the wisdom, and keep going.

Another obstacle to confidence can occur when a person is overly attached to being seen, heard, understood, or validated by someone else. If you function in this manner, it is likely that you will not perceive your own value. You may even feel wronged or powerless when others do not acknowledge or seem interested in you. If you find yourself disheartened when another person does not acknowledge or show an interest in your ideas, feelings, needs, or accomplishments, it is an opportunity for you to validate yourself. Others are often not really capable of doing that and are not responsible for you. Whatever you desire from another person is inside of you. If you can perceive it, then it is within your own capabilities. For instance, when you want someone else to understand or validate something about you, you have already perceived value and understand whatever it is that you want them to acknowledge because you have first acknowledged it in yourself. Therefore, you don't need to receive this from anyone else because you already have it. Simply celebrate it by acknowledging what you've identified within your own experience, values, or capabilities. Some examples might be, "Yes, I do participate with values" or "I do understand the significance of this" or "The idea that I have is inspiring!" Feel the experience and value of what you are stating. In this way it becomes integrated as an experiential knowing.

As you proceed through the stages of confidence building, it is possible to become overly attached to what you learn within certain areas of development. This can bring about dependency on it and self-righteousness. Be careful that you do not over-identify with a role or set idea about yourself. I will give you an example of this in the following story.

This situation involved a minister by the name of Pastor Jim. In his childhood, he experienced abuse from his parents. Through the need to overcome the suffering he turned to his belief in God. The inner seeking led him to greater personal understanding and spiritual awareness. Jim wanted to share what he had learned with others, so he began to teach. It was through the teaching that he developed social skills, and then realized that he wanted to be the pastor of a church. His sermons were insightful, and he was a good teacher. Pastor Jim's belief in perfectionism required him to believe that he was the very best preacher. A strong confidence was developed with his abilities as a spiritual leader; however, he did not learn to fully trust in himself beyond that role. He had an ongoing need for validation from others. At some point during most of his sermons, he would compare himself to other church leaders in a judgmental manner. His criticism of others made him feel superior, and his congregation believed what he said. He saw himself as a confident person but didn't realize

Transitioning Beyond Your Conditioned Blueprint

that it was unbalanced, incomplete confidence. He had to put himself in a grandiose position to feel confident. This came about through his unconscious desire to contain and possess his knowledge. He habitually gave his insights over to his mind. This allowed his ego to maintain a hold on him. Deep down he believed that if another preacher was perceived as more skilled than he was, then he might lose some of his worth or credibility. He would temporarily feel threatened – unable to recognize equality within individuality. His ego provided him with false validation through a belief in his superiority; however, he could not perceive what was happening. He had not fully worked through his dependency for validation and approval from others. His habitual participation in this domineering behavior kept him from realizing himself as an equal within the diversity of all people and creation.

Because every individual is unique, no one can ever be like or replace another person. There is always something to learn and receive from every person. All people have their own particular strengths, inadequacies, skills, and awareness. These are gifts in the ever-changing experience of being human. Beyond the ego level of attachment and resistance, there is Divine oneness connecting everyone and all things.

Can you identify any situations of dependency and false confidence in yourself? If so, write down the details.

_____
_____
_____
_____
_____
_____
_____
_____
_____
_____
_____
_____
_____
_____
_____

First, you must see and validate yourself. Embrace what is valuable to you so that you are not competing for or dependent upon validation from others. To be more tolerant and accepting of others, it is helpful to be curious about them instead of judgmental. See other people as they are instead of the way that you think that they should be. Notice when you are comparing yourself to someone else. Respect your own unique individuality as well as that of others. Know that there will be ongoing opportunities for you to build upon your strengths and abilities. There will always be more for you to realize and learn.

In what ways do you need to accept yourself and let go of a tendency to compare, compete, or feel superior?

Transitioning Beyond Your Conditioned Blueprint

The next example involved a young woman named Emily, who lived alone and was quite comfortable in her own company. She was a forward thinker, curious and courageous, who stood out as different. When she was alone, she appreciated herself; however, in certain social situations, she tended to compare herself to other people with the idea that maybe she should be like them. This created self-doubt and limited her confidence.

In one situation, she was in a coffee shop listening to several young women talking about topics that she hadn't considered discussing. They shared intimate details about themselves and the people who were close to them. While listening, she began to doubt her social skills and abilities. Emily imagined that maybe she was not normal – that something must be lacking in her because she wasn't having the same types of conversations with other women. The idea tormented her for days to the point of her feeling sad and alone. Finally, her suffering led her to question the way that she was engaging with herself. She contemplated the judgments that her ego had been tossing around. She recognized them to be faulty destructive beliefs and let them go. Her self-inquiry led her to realize how often her own mind had been the problem – not the situation or other people. She concluded that she did not have any true interest in sharing the subject matter that was discussed by the other women in the coffee shop. Through contemplation she had successfully transitioned herself out of fantasy and conflict and into a more authentic experience with greater self-acceptance. The contemplation brought understanding and the understanding brought confidence.

Fragmented focus and ideas that we should all be the same can result in a sense of lack. Through comparison and self-judgment, Emily was temporarily blinded and separated from her own truths. On the flip side, the self-created suffering served as a doorway for greater personal understanding. Through participation in curiosity and inner inquiry, the untruths as well as the value of all experiences can be realized.

Can you identify any areas of self-doubt that were developed from the habit of comparison, association with sameness, or self-judgment? If so, write down the details.

_____
_____
_____
_____
_____
_____
_____

Transitioning Beyond Your Conditioned Blueprint

Now, use your curiosity and contemplation skills while focusing on the self-doubt to see what else you can discover. You might ask yourself, "What kind of situations activate this struggle? What are the beliefs associated with it? What beliefs, reactions, etc. need to be challenged, and in what way can I take new steps toward change?" As your view broadens, you will become aware of multi-layered faulty beliefs, resistance, and behaviors that create limitations as well as new possibilities for change. Now, are you willing to make a commitment to walk through faulty beliefs or resistance, take new action, and expand in your personal confidence? Contemplate this.

Once you develop more confidence, your tendency and attempts to function in the same way as others will diminish; however, you will still need to be aware the possibility of it. Sometimes the uncovering of truth is not so simple. An attachment to the idea that we all have to be the same can be hidden within layers of various behaviors. Unraveling it may require a committed, vigilant state of curiosity and presence. Through presence you will see, understand, discover new options, and have the space to choose differently.

Chapter Eight

Comparison, Belief in Sameness, and Compliance

-25-

The act of comparison reinforces expectations of sameness

The act of comparison often carries the suggestion that others should function like you do, or that you should be like them. Sometimes people make comparisons as a way to feel superior to others.

Unhealthy comparison leads to expectations of conformity, fixed rules, competition, envy, judgment, blame, projected or internalized guilt, co-dependency, or the need for superiority. Unhealthy comparison gives camouflage to these behaviors. Sameness comes from the ego's black and white thinking and the need to predict reality instead of being fully present to discover. When you are in presence, you experience the everchanging diversity of each moment as it unfolds. Think of each experience as a wave. Waves can arise in various sizes and shapes, then they glide along until their completion. At that time, they settle back into the substance from which they came with a moment of stillness before the next one arises. No two waves are ever exactly alike. Belief in and the expectation of sameness is one of the most predominant illusions of mankind. Diversity is the natural rule of life. When people depend upon the illusion of sameness, it will lead to competition, dependency, self-doubt, judgment, a sense of separation, and struggle.

On the other hand, comparisons can be used in a healthy manner to bring about awareness and understanding of differences. When used without judgment or expectations of sameness, comparison can broaden your awareness of the vast diversity of life.

The next example involved a woman named Belinda who suffers with many layers of unbalanced behavior. These included a belief in sameness, fear of being judged, the practice of comparison, compliance, judgment of herself and others, and identification with drama. As a result, she had little self-awareness or confidence. She lived in a hierarchal struggle and could not embrace the diversity of individuality. She used drama to maintain the illusion of control, to shift responsibility for herself onto others, and to have those people temporarily carry her inadequacies. In this way, her own internalized fear of self, others, and life could appear to be outside in other people, instead of inside herself.

Belinda carried a blueprint of false shame that had been passed down through many generations. She had unmet needs from a lack of being seen, understood, or nurtured as a child. This was due to her mother Gloria, who routinely bullied, judged, shamed, and demeaned her throughout her childhood.

Belinda was adopted. Gloria frequently made comments about how lucky her daughter was to have been adopted. Gloria felt that her sacrifice in adopting of a child was monumental, and that Belinda's gratitude should match it. Gloria was stern and shamed Belinda around having needs or making mistakes. She suggested that Belinda should show her appreciation by making her mother happy and not making any mistakes. Gloria expected her daughter's perceptions and responses to be consistently and exactly the same as what she expected. Because Gloria was unable to participate with Belinda on a spontaneous human level, Belinda never learned the skills for directly and authentically sharing or processing things that felt meaningful or personally challenging. She was afraid of being found out to be wrong even though she was constantly told that she was wrong. Because of this, Belinda constantly tried to be compliant and fulfill the expectations of others. She was dependent upon their approval. She did not feel safe without it. Their approval was her only known predictable foundation for stability. She felt loved when she experienced approval; otherwise, she felt alone. Her primary emotion was anxiety, but she did not consciously know why she was afraid. The relationship with her mother indoctrinated her into a pattern of self-denial, accepting unacceptable behavior from others, being submissive to another's anger, pretending that she was okay when she was not, and living her life through the theme of pleasing others at her own expense. She was co-dependent.

When Belinda became an adult and had children of her own, she was confused about what to do with her feelings and needs. Because she did not know how to navigate them with others, she did not directly participate on this level with her husband or children. Her unmet needs and feelings remained for the most part inside of her along with her childhood beliefs which fostered a sense of fear toward others, fear of her authentic self, and feelings of isolation, rejection, and abandonment. She also judged any personal tendency toward a natural process just as harshly as her mother had done. Periodically, when there was no room left for any more internal emotional build up, she would act out the accumulated feelings in an exaggerated manner while blaming others for not recognizing her needs. She would suggest that they should have known what was needed – that her children should feel guilt for not seeing and acting to remedy her own inner turmoil and satisfy her unmet needs. She was unconsciously doing to her children what her mother unconsciously did to her.

When this happened, the children would not see it coming because they were so mentally and emotionally suppressed themselves. There was no process leading up to the outburst, so the children would feel confused, judged, guilted, and trapped in the experience of being made to feel wrong with no means for resolving it. The unconscious goal of Belinda's outburst was to get others to merge with it, process it as their own, and thereby take responsibility for it. But it was not possible for her children to take the turmoil from their mother and make it their own. As a result, they would end up believing that they were somehow wrong and responsible for the mother's displaced emotions while being left with feelings of inadequacy, internalized self-judgment and guilt over it. It was as if Belinda had unloaded all her tumultuous feelings into them. There was an unconscious partial transfer and acceptance of the suffering from the mother to the children. The transfer was fueled by suggestions of blame and shame. It reinforced self-doubt in all participants. Although it gave Belinda temporary relief from her suffering, it was not a solution, so the cycle endlessly repeated itself.

Transitioning Beyond Your Conditioned Blueprint

Since Belinda did not have an effective means for participating with her own feelings and needs, she was unable to acknowledge or navigate the needs of her children. She responded to their feelings and needs with resistance, judgment, blame, and rejection. She perceived them as a burden. Some of her children learned what she had learned and replicated it to some degree in their own behavior. The patterns got passed down from generation to generation.

When someone believes or expects another person to have the same feelings, perspectives, or approach in life as themselves, they are denying that other person's right to be an individual. The recipient learns to put their spontaneous needs, perspectives, and option for choosing in the background. They master the ability to pretend. They gain a false confidence by fulfilling the needs and solving the problems of other people. Their behavior becomes compulsive while providing limited confidence that is dependent upon a role. When this is the case, the person needs to learn a process for self-awareness, discerning truth from fantasy, recognizing individual boundaries, participating for discovery, and negotiating vast possibilities or circumstances with self and others. A more comprehensive sense of confidence and trust is created through direct, conscious, authentic participation with all the variables within oneself and life.

Can you relate to any of what has been described? Do you recognize any similar experience in your life circumstances or in your behaviors? If so, describe the details.

_____
_____
_____
_____
_____
_____
_____
_____
_____
_____
_____
_____

A process for discerning truth from fantasy, individuality, and boundaries between yourself and others

1. Begin a daily practice of bringing your focus inward to clearly experience what is true and untrue. Create a routine so that inner witnessing and discovery becomes a regular, familiar part of your life.
2. When you see yourself pretending, notice the content of it, such as the beliefs, fears, your needs, and what you are getting from the behavior.
3. Notice any tendency to suppress or resist direct participation outside of your conditioned roles.
4. Notice any tendency to conform for the purpose of avoiding unjust blame and shame. Know that when you compulsively conform, your individuality and authentic experience are made invisible. If you don't respect yourself, then others will not be given the chance to do so either.

Transitioning Beyond Your Conditioned Blueprint

5. You will likely be afraid to participate in new ways. Do not wait for the fear to go away – walk through it. If the compulsive fear decides for you, then you will be feeding it and giving it support.
6. When you see your thoughts or feelings slip into the background, pull them back into your field of focus. Decide whether immediate attention should be given to your needs. For instance, would it help to communicate something about them or not? Do you need to offer a statement about your position? Do you need to ask some questions? Do you need to create a boundary?
7. Initially you will need to use your *will* to stay focused in your own perspectives, needs, and preferred options.
8. When it comes time to share a need, share it in a direct clean manner without processing the other person. If you put one toe in the water while trying to feel out what the other person's response will be, then your focus will once again be on them instead of you sharing yourself. Also, it will not be useful to tell the other person how they should think or feel in response to what you share. Simply share while allowing some space for the other person to process and offer a response. In this way, your understanding of possibilities will be clearer. Through their response or lack of one, you will discover their capabilities.
9. Share your thoughts, feelings, needs, or perspectives directly while using a curious tone as opposed to a serious one. Think of it as an offering. Someone else may or may not be capable of receiving it. A curious tone is non-threatening and invites others to participate. It will also help you to feel safer.
10. Use words that will provide a clear understanding of your inner experience. You are exploring to see if there is a possibility for mutual participation. A person's response to your sharing will give you a lot of information about them. You will also discover whether or not you can be understood by that person.
11. Through your sharing, you will have a chance to experience yourself participating with what you know is true for you in an individual process. This will serve to validate your ongoing experience and create individual responsibility.

12. If you are afraid of being seen as wrong, decide for yourself whether your experience is valuable to you. If so, internally own it. When you stay anchored in what is purposeful and true for you, then it will not feel diminished by another person's perspectives when they do not understand or agree. No one else can decide for you.
13. Avoid using blame, judgment, or ideas of should be or could be in your communications. These approaches will only muddy the individual experience and confuse boundaries.
14. When you witness turmoil in another person, your past approach may have been to attempt to process the other person's experience or help them to become happy so that you could be comfortable. This is a disguised form of control. Plus, when you process or repeatedly see the way for another person, you are likely enabling them in a powerless, needy, or inferior state. When you become invested in another person's experience to the extent of processing it as if it were yours, you are crossing boundaries. Sometimes other people do not want your input. Only give it if someone else is sincerely asking for your help – not to simply feed their internal drama or to make yourself feel good.
15. If you are unclear about something, ask questions from a position of curiosity for the purpose of discovering and for the understanding of yourself and others. Contemplate new information to see how it may be beneficial or not and where further exploration or boundaries may be needed.
16. Often, what comes from an interaction will not be what you expected. This is the natural way of life. Sameness is an illusion.
17. Practice every day. Your new process of discovery and participation will become more and more natural.

Now write down what you have learned. Have you gained more clarity about how your behaviors create problems for you? What steps can you take for further discovery or to create change?

_____
_____
_____
_____

Transitioning Beyond Your Conditioned Blueprint

-26-

Understanding self-doubt and lack of confidence

Self-doubt most often originates from a lack of experience in particular areas of one's life. Sometimes it is anchored in a fear of not knowing or of being wrong. This can come from repeated criticism from a parent, teacher, a bully, etc. early in life or a narcissistic boss later in life. *Criticism reinforces an identity in harmful beliefs or ideas about oneself, whereas direct participation and discovery in the ongoing experiences of life supports growth and change.* Harmful beliefs can be broad, encompassing large areas of a person's life, or be limited to one type of situation. One example would be when a person fears conflict because they believe that they should know all of the answers.

A faulty belief that is often present in this instance is the idea that to not know is to be wrong and that being perfect is a requirement for acceptance from others. To believe that one should always know is to believe that no new discovery or learning can take place. The experience becomes rule based rather than discovery based. In actuality, each time a person does not know something, it opens a doorway for more discovery and provides access into the substance of life. Each time a person does not know something, they have the chance to participate in something new. Confidence cannot be developed without direct, courageous participation in life. When a person retreats from the unknown or the possibility of conflict, they will likely find themselves pretending rather than seeking information, understanding, or possibilities for resolution. This comes from black and white, right/wrong, dominant/submissive, fragmented programming. It distracts a person from being fully present. Instead of directly participating with life, a person will interact with set rules or imaginary scenarios in their mind that

Transitioning Beyond Your Conditioned Blueprint

most often only terrorize them. The person ends up experiencing what they most fear by their own hand. So, what is the solution for transforming this?

If you have this problem, the first step is to bring your focus inward to purposefully recognize your own fears and beliefs. If you continue to pretend or deny what is there, you will be feeding your fears and unhealthy imagination. When a fear arises, see it as an offering from your subconscious. You can remain as the observer instead of jumping into any distractive feeling or thought form. Then activate some curiosity to discern fantasy scenarios and faulty beliefs. Next, ask yourself questions about how your psyche is benefitting or not from any faulty beliefs. When you realize that a compulsive behavior is not purposeful, say no to it. From within a curious state, seek to discover new steps for direct courageous participation in the present moment. Apply the wisdom that you discover, create boundaries, and participate with purpose. You will discover that life provides a never-ending stream of opportunities for learning more and purposeful sharing.

Chapter Nine

An In-depth View of Anger and Judgment

-27-

Participation with judgment, anger, and fixed ideas is sometimes used to dominate and control others.

Expecting others to conform to one's fixed ideas is sometimes the largest part of a person's identity. This next example involved a man named John who functioned within generational patterns of judgment, anger, and fixed ideas that were used to diminish, dominate, and aggressively force his wishes onto others.

John was rejected by his father Bill. Because John came from an unplanned, unwanted pregnancy, his father never accepted him. His father was dismissive of him yet embraced the other children. From the time of his birth onward, John was relentlessly criticized and judged by his father, creating ongoing stress in the household. Because John's mother rarely challenged her husband's behavior, the love that she gave to her son was unable to counteract the effects of the abuse. The siblings experienced inner conflict from their inability to know what to do about the suffering of their brother, so they simply ignored it. Their solution was to make him feel special when he complained. He soon believed that if he complained, then some people would give him positive attention – he felt accepted and loved. He was not given any examples of how to navigate or process a harmful experience in a healthy manner. He felt angry, sad, overburdened, trapped, and powerless while in the presence of his father.

John interpreted his father's dominance in several ways. The dominant person seemed to be safe, and the person being dominated seemed to be in danger. Since John had not learned a process for navigating his father's bullying behavior, his dysfunctional understanding of it was black and white – it was either/or with no alternate options. He identified with a dominant angry role for a sense of safety when in the face of conflict or any anticipation of it. Then to get a sense of caring from others, he complained while presenting himself as a victim. He unconsciously knew that it would get him the attention that he craved.

Over time, the rewards from his complaining diminished. With this, he became more and more dependent upon telling malicious, over-the-top, harmful stories about others while diabolically choosing his victims. His targets were with those who appeared to be either the weakest and most vulnerable or the most intelligent. He felt threatened by intelligence. He arranged circumstances so that his victim had little to no effective defense. When other people united in John's self-created dramas, he felt accepted and powerful. However, the behavior had to be endlessly repeated.

John took the programming from his upbringing into adulthood. He married, had many children, and none of them were from planned pregnancies. He was a dismissive, domineering, critical parent who fabricated reasons to reject all of his children. He took on a position within the dominant dynamic that he subconsciously believed to be the safest for himself. He was always right – no one else's feelings, perspectives, needs, goals, or confidence were allowed in his presence. Everyone in the household was expected to follow his lead and expectations at all costs. They had to become an extension of his demands. When certain family members allied with his abuse of others, they were praised and accepted. Because he was dependent upon his success in controlling other people, he had little confidence in himself and his ability to honestly navigate life. If he was not in charge, a sense of powerlessness would send him into a state of rage and drama as he sought to regain control. For him to feel safe, he needed others to mold themselves to his expectations and comfort level. He needed them to be submissive at all costs or function as an ally to dominate others on his behalf. He perceived individuality, the process of discovery, truth, and another person's self-confidence to be a threat. If any of this surfaced in one of his children, he judged it and sought to destroy it.

Transitioning Beyond Your Conditioned Blueprint

In an attempt to consistently dominate others, he incorporated his desires and judgments about how others should participate with his self-created rules. These rules were made to serve his comfort, so that he would not be challenged by the experiences of others or be required to take responsibility for his own actions. He was not capable of navigating real life experiences, so he had to condense them down into a framework of rule-based fantasy to feel safe. He had no effective, safe functional programming for the recognition or navigation of the individual variables of people or situations.

As a result of this, some of his children were not able to establish a foundation for intimacy, curiosity, or the ability to participate directly and honestly in relationships with others. They could not fully recognize or participate with their own abilities, likes, dislikes, goals, or effectively solve problems. They did not learn how to create healthy boundaries or participate with honest, respectful choices of yes and no. Most of them perceived authority as a threat – as something that could be used to gain power over them or to take away what they valued – even if they didn't know what that was. It would leave them feeling trapped in a powerless, unsafe position. Some of them learned to use dominant roles against others. In response to not knowing, as adults, they would bully other people, flee from conflict, isolate, become hostile, become compliant, pretend that experiences were not happening, dissociate, compete, or create dramas – anything to avoid direct participation. As you can see, all of these behaviors came from a place of incomplete learning, black and white thinking, and a struggle to attain some sense of safety, even though it was only a false and temporary sense of safety.

These adults, were to various degrees, indoctrinated into domineering or submissive behaviors. Their behavioral blueprints became a frame of reference for processing life. However, a few of them did persevere and transition through the limitations, suffering, and faulty programming. They developed personal awareness, gained wisdom, and transitioned into greater presence. They were able to change by using curiosity, direct inquiry, and participation. They learned to discern the difference between truth and fantasy, to recognize the option of choice, and to learn how to purposefully navigate life. With these individuals, their recurring suffering was the impetus for seeking something healthier and igniting curiosity within. They were committed to testing the ongoing possibilities of life while making healthy use of the *will* and *fierceness*.

Once a person learns how to discern the difference between fantasy and truth, then they can apply healthy yeses and noes to life. The option is available all for people to embrace a self-discovery process, to find the courage to directly experience life, and seek something more than what they have learned. They must practice participating with their new realizations until the old patterns are mostly or all gone. The possibility of present moment participation with life is innate in everyone. The requirements for success may include a strong commitment to overcome the suffering, a childlike state of innocent curiosity, surrender, the decision to let go of what you think you already know while inviting discoveries from within the unknown, and a willingness to walk through fear to test new possibilities and integrate wisdom.

What the two previous examples have in common is an approach to life that is based on rigid ideas or fixed rules. In each representation, there is an unconscious compulsive effort to transfer one person's experience onto other people. Each human being is a unique individual, so this is only possible when someone does not understand what is happening and how to be curious and discover through presence. When such behaviors are passed on, they create a generational experience of powerlessness and suffering with internalized or outward expressions of cyclical unhealthy behaviors. These types of patterns can exist to a greater or lesser degree. Not all situations are as extreme as these previous two examples.

Do you recognize any anger-driven domineering patterns within yourself? Are you afraid of anger or do you feel powerless in the presence of someone who uses anger to force their beliefs and perspectives onto others? Do you use anger to demand that others think and feel in the same ways as you?

Write down the details of your perceptions, understanding, or realizations.

_____
_____
_____
_____
_____
_____

Transitioning Beyond Your Conditioned Blueprint

-28-

Transformational steps for the aggressor

If you are the aggressor who uses anger, judgment, and self-created rules to deny the individuality of others, then the following transformative steps may be helpful.

1. Practice inner witnessing on a daily basis. When anger, judgment, entitlement, envy, or the desire to dominate arise, observe it within yourself rather than attaching it to other people. Through this process you will be giving it the space to transform. Do not try to make anything happen, just observe it. If you create a struggle with it, you will be closing up the space that the witnessing created. As you proceed, your insight and understanding will arise naturally. Once you have some space to observe, you have the option to become curious. The space of witnessing and open-ended curiosity will invite understanding into your experience.
2. Recognize that change is only possible when you understand and take responsibility for what you are doing. Therefore, you must seek to understand your behavior and the effects that it has upon yourself and others.
3. Know that your actions have become compulsive at this point. The anger is an unconscious addiction. Participation in it feels satisfying because it is predictable; it provides a dominant role; and your body is releasing hits of dopamine in response to it. Know that it also creates separation from the possibility of authentically shared experience with others and puts you in an endless struggle with a win/lose dynamic. When you are successful in triggering others, you become merged with the negative

energy of a shared struggle. However, you have a choice to learn something more and live life with more meaning.
4. A daily practice of inner witnessing is also necessary for recognizing the difference between fact and fantasy, cause and effect, and authentic individuality.
5. Because of early exposure to criticism and anger or coddling, you likely feel afraid of being wrong, feeling stuck in shame, and spontaneously experiencing others in ways as different from yourself. If you are not functioning in your addictive angry role, you may feel as though you are naked. You will discover with practice that without the anger addiction, you are free from bondage.
6. It is important to witness any reactions as they arise. When you judge or formulate rules toward others, notice when a desire arises to aggressively impose those judgments or rules upon other people and blame them for being wrong. Refrain from doing it. Seek to understand what that behavior has been doing for you and to you. Use your curiosity.
7. Notice when you feel emotionally reactive toward people who are different from you. Recognize any tendency to judge them as being wrong. Notice when you have a desire to compete with them, to make them feel shameful, or to dominate their experience with your set ideas while wanting them to be compliant or feel inferior. When you see this occur, contemplate it rather than continuing to act out toward other people. Take responsibility for your thoughts and patterns by accepting them as yours rather than making excuses for your behavior, blaming, or making up stories. Recognize how damaging it has been for yourself and others.
8. Stop blaming others for breaking your rules. If you get stuck in blame, you will be positioning yourself into a dependent state. Blame is not purposeful. Blame creates and supports a state of struggle. It will also encourage ongoing anger.
9. Put yourself in a curious state while seeking to understand the individuality and unique process in other people. Everyone's process will be different than yours. This is because each person has their own unique history which leads them to have individual abilities, perspectives,

feelings, approaches, likes, dislikes, needs, challenges, goals, fears, and knowledge.
10. Practice asking other people questions for the purpose of discovering who they are. Do not ask questions that have been infused with your personal perspective. Instead ask open ended questions. They will not have any suggestions added to them.
11. Do not judge or criticize what other people have shared with you. If you don't like what they've shared, do not call them names in an attempt to dominate their perspectives and emotions. Thank them for sharing. Notice where your perceptions are similar and where they are different. Respect the differences. Refrain from any attempts to process for the person.
12. Refrain from being sarcastic. Sarcasm is an unconscious attempt to dominate others with criticism or belittling which has been wrapped in humor. It is a form of bullying.
13. Recognize where real individual and shared possibilities exist which are based in truth – not fantasy or desires. Actual facts are based in direct experience or details that you have witnessed over and over again. The facts have not been infused with or embellished with stories, judgments, assumptions, or reactions that came from your personal desires.
14. Accept the reality that one distorted detail cannot define a whole situation or another person's identity.
15. Be courageous. If you have been or are causing pain or suffering to another person, seek to understand why you are doing it, how it limits you and prevents you from perceiving your own individuality, its negative effects on others, how it shuts off the possibility of authentic intimacy, and closes off possibilities for learning. When you understand the depth of what has occurred, it is important to take responsibility for it, have compassion, and apologize. You must feel the truth of this; otherwise, it is meaningless. This is when the wisdom of the total experience can be anchored in your psyche. This will also provide some familiarity when a need arises to be receptive and learn more while in a vulnerable situation. When you perceive from a basis of truth, while taking

responsibility and making new choices, you will be developing some trust and confidence for participating in the unknown.
16. Validate yourself while respecting the individuality of others. Other people are not responsible for validating you by conforming or going along with you.
17. Know that every person is unique. Sameness cannot apply. There will be similarities that come and go; however, no one is or can be the same as you.

-29-

Transformational steps for the recipient of aggression

If you are the recipient of another person's aggression, anger, judgment, lack of boundaries, and fantasy-based rules, the following transformative steps may be helpful.

1. Practice inner witnessing on a daily basis. When you feel self-doubt, are afraid of retribution for being seen as wrong, are afraid of being falsely blamed or shamed, have the desire to please, an urgency to fix, etc., observe it within yourself rather than acting it out in a conditioned role by being compliant, dissociating, or accepting a state of a struggle. This mental/emotional struggle is made up of multi-layered compulsive reactions, suppressed needs, and faulty beliefs. Know that you do not have to take on a compliant or submissive role in response to the untruths of others. Simply see the truth as it is and witness your own enabling tendencies. Also, contemplate to recognize your own option of choice when another person attempts to dominate or decide things for you through aggressive words or actions.
2. If you are targeted by the aggressor and feel powerless, you may possibly retreat into yourself while engaging in unpleasant defensive scenarios. This endless cyclical practice will feed your sense of powerlessness. Recognize what this is and say NO to it. Use your discernment to identify truth, to take purposeful actions which support your well-being, or create

boundaries. Do not pretend that the unacceptable is okay or you will end up violating your own boundaries of personal integrity.

3. When you unconsciously conform or please others and then are validated for conforming by the abuser, your body releases hits of dopamine. The act of receiving the reward brings this about. This is because you perceive the act of compliance to bring approval and safety when in reality it can cause harm. It can make you overlook abuse or controlling behavior from others and become attached to *hopeful fantasies* of the other person suddenly caring about, understanding, and accepting you. False hope distorts truth and invites ongoing unhealthy experiences. If you have repeatedly seen the same behavior from the same person, then your hopeful wishes are likely only a fantasy.

4. Therefore, a daily practice of inner witnessing is necessary for recognizing the difference between fact and fantasy, cause and effect, and individual experience.

5. Recognize that change is only possible when you understand and take responsibility for what you are doing. Therefore, you must seek to understand your behavior and the way that it affects you and others. If you continue in the habitual patterns, it will give others permission to keep doing what they've been doing. It enables them.

6. If you find yourself trying to convince the aggressor that their perception or behavior is wrong, know that it is likely a waste of time. Instead own what you see as the truth. Validate the truth for yourself while speaking it when it serves a purpose. Otherwise, refrain. When possible, remove yourself from the situation. The more you practice, the easier this will become.

7. Because of early exposure to criticism and anger, you likely feel afraid of being wrong, being stuck in blame or shame, and spontaneously experiencing yourself without the predictable confines of false safety provided by conforming and pretending. Those conditioned behaviors most likely got created in childhood when no other options were available except to submit.

8. Notice when you feel self-doubt while in the presence of others. Recognize a tendency to fear the possibility of them judging you or

Transitioning Beyond Your Conditioned Blueprint

perceiving you as wrong. Notice any urgency to comply to avoid feeling unsafe or shamed. Notice when you are adjusting your behavior according to the expectations that you imagine others may have of you. Do you emotionally prepare yourself for imagined criticism, judgment, or potential harm from others? Do you believe that you must endure bad behavior from others while pretending that you are not being affected? Do you make up scenarios in response to these imaginings?

9. When you notice any of these responses in yourself, contemplate them rather than jumping into them. If you've already immersed yourself into them, then internally take a step back while witnessing your mind and emotions. This can be accomplished by stating what you see occurring. Use your own name when doing this. For example, "I see Julia adjusting her behavior to comply and pretend that nothing abusive is going on." Using your own name while witnessing is an effective way to create space. In this way you will realize that the behavior is not your identity. It is conditioning and you are learning how to be aware of it and make alternate choices. Once you have the space, contemplate to access greater understanding and new choices. Take responsibility for your thoughts and conditioned patterns by accepting them as yours rather than making excuses for your enabling behavior, blaming, or making up stories.

10. If you get stuck in blame, you will be positioning yourself in a dependent state. Blame is not purposeful. Blame creates and supports a state of struggle. Instead participate with honesty, create boundaries, make new choices from real possibilities rather than waiting for a fantasy to materialize. Recognize how damaging your historical approach has been for yourself and how it has enabled others.

11. When interacting with others who are aggressive, put yourself in a curious state and witness the individuality in them. Do not try to figure them out by analyzing; just see them as they are. As you participate, they will be showing you who they are. Do not become attached to understanding their behavior in a rational manner – sometimes you have to accept that what you see is irrational. Notice any tendency to project hopeful fantasies onto them, and then remind yourself of the history.

Practice stepping out of the urgency to please others. Recognize their experience as separate from yours. Your individuality, needs, and process will be different from that of other people. You are unique just as they are. Do not defend or try to prove yourself. Share your thoughts, feelings, and process for the purpose of offering understanding that may or may not be received. Accept the fact that you can see yourself, and if others cannot, then it is out of your hands. Do not try to force a connection when direct experience has shown you that it is not there. You do not need approval from others to be yourself. Each person has their own unique history that shapes their perspectives, approaches, likes, dislikes, challenges, abilities, and knowledge.

12. Practice asking people questions for the purpose of discovering their individuality and capabilities. Use curiosity to anchor yourself. Do not ask questions that have been infused with your personal perspectives. This includes you adding suggestions about how you think the other person should process. Instead ask open ended questions. Your questions will not have any suggestions of any kind added into them. Seek to understand the other person's experience without personalizing it.

13. Do not judge or criticize yourself when others attempt to reject or diminish what you have shared. Celebrate your sharing. You are the only one who can decide the value of your experience. When others share with you, thank them for sharing. Notice where your perceptions are similar and where they are different. Respect the differences. Refrain from making assumptions or attempting to process for other people. If you are still unclear about their answers, ask more questions. Verbalize your understanding of what you heard back to the person who shared it with you. In this way, you are confirming your perceptions and letting the other person know if they were heard and understood or not.

14. Recognize where real individual and shared possibilities exist which are based in truth – facts – not desires. Actual facts are based in direct experience or with things that you have witnessed over and over again. The facts have not been infused with stories, judgments, or reactions to personal desires. In each new situation the details, information, and understanding that you perceive will change.

15. When in conflict with others be fully present. Be courageous. Take a confident position in truth and be flexible enough to see beyond your habitual ways of interacting. Let others know when they are being inappropriate with you. If they have been causing you pain or suffering, seek to understand your own beliefs, how they limit you, and prevent you from perceiving your own individuality. Make note of your history of enabling, how this shuts off the possibility of authentic intimacy, and closes off possibilities for learning. When you understand the depth of what has occurred, it is important to firmly say no when something is inappropriate and contemplate what is real for you as an individual. This is when the wisdom of your experience can be anchored into your psyche. This will also provide you with a natural opportunity to learn more through direct experience when in a vulnerable situation. When you perceive from a basis of truth while taking responsibility and choosing for yourself, you will be developing some trust and confidence in your ability to participate in the unknown.
16. Know that you are not responsible for validating others by conforming or going along with them. If the situation offers mutual sharing opportunities, remain open and try to listen and understand. Otherwise, create compassionate boundaries.
17. You must refrain from letting your mind decide any timeframe for your discovery process or to judge your progress. Both of those things will close the space for witnessing. As you proceed, insight and understanding naturally arise.
18. Realize that every person is unique. People are not uniform. Their similarities will come and go.

-30-

How to overcome self-judgment and deal with judgment from others while building inner strength and confidence

Perhaps the self-judgment occurs in response to negative criticisms or inappropriate behavior that has been aimed at you. It may also be happening because you first judged yourself and then imagined someone else to be judging you. In this case, you would be projecting the idea of them judging or rejecting you; however, you would be the one doing the judging and reacting within your own imagination while pretending that it was coming from someone else. When judgment is taking place, notice the following: Do you feel as though you can't be yourself, or have your own thoughts, needs, or beliefs unless someone else understands, agrees with, or believes in you? If you do believe any of that you will likely judge yourself and imagine others to be doing it too. However, there will be times when you do experience direct judgment from another person. This can happen when someone else compares him or herself to you and then feels rejection, envy, or entitlement. If you buy into someone else's suggestions or your own unconscious patterns of judgment, you will likely become defensive, angry, sad, or disempowered. If you had self-doubt to begin with, then the other person's suggestions will act to remind you of what was already there. In this case, bring your focus inward to explore any faulty beliefs behind your self-doubt. Then say no to it while recognizing yourself as a unique individual. Your unique experience belongs to you; another person cannot decide its value. Only you can decide its value. When you stand confidently in your own beliefs and needs, while taking responsibility for yourself, you will naturally choose what fits for you in your own life.

For the possibility of change, you must recognize what part of the judgment is yours and what part of it is coming from elsewhere. Judgment creates anger, sadness, blame, dependency, and many other destructive reactive emotions. If you are assuming or imagining someone else to be judging you, then all that you can know for sure is that it is in your own head. You can be sure that someone is judging you if you experience it coming from them directly. Direct experience means that they spoke words of judgment, or perhaps they displayed a facial expression of disapproval, or projected palpable feelings of judgment, etc. It is important to recognize that when this behavior comes from another person, it is inside of them. It came from their mind, from their behavior patterns, and their personal history. It's about their own beliefs, reactions, and programming. It is not about you even when they try to make it about you, so do not take it in by attaching a role to it. Do not become a diminished version of yourself by feeling inferior, defensive, or dependent. Examples of this might be if you respond by feeling bad about yourself, shrinking away, being outwardly reactive, creating a drama after the fact, or trying to convince someone of your worth. If you become defensive, then you will have taken on an inferior role. If you get stuck on this level, you may find yourself engaged in negative imaginary stories and scenarios. What I'm speaking about here is an unconscious pattern that was created as a defense. However, it will not be effective for bringing about inner peace, real life resolutions, or confidence. Judgments lead to compulsive thoughts and emotions; the compulsive emotions lead to reaction stories. Once this cycle is created, a person may get caught in it and not know how to transition beyond it.

You can challenge any self-judgment through inner witnessing, seeking to understand the beliefs within the behavior, discerning individual identity for yourself, and acknowledging what you see in the other person. Contemplate what you discover so that the truth of it becomes anchored. Accept what you experience for the time being. Then redirect your focus into choices that support the truth. Engage in self-validation, create direct truth-based communications, and set personal boundaries. In order to do this effectively on a regular basis, you will need to get into the habit of personal observation and discerning truth from fantasy so that you can create inner boundaries with your own behavior. This simply means that you will be watching your own mental/emotional reactions as they occur rather than unconsciously getting drawn into them. When you watch what arises from the unconsciousness, you will not be jumping into it, adding any details, or playing a reactive role in response to what you see. The more you do this, the more you will be creating space and a sense of distance from your compulsive thoughts and reactions. This is an important process to learn – one that you can develop through committed ongoing practice. Curiosity is a key component of this.

When sharing with others, if you offer something of yourself through a curious state, then you will be providing a safe invitation for others to participate. Curiosity has a certain innocence to it. The possibility of being heard and understood is dramatically increased. Curiosity creates a space of receptivity. When engaging through a state of curiosity there is no specific expectation. If something or nothing comes back to you it is okay. If another person is receptive, they may become curious in response to your questions. If a person is not receptive, then they will probably not extend that curiosity back to you. Just accept what is and is not possible and make appropriate choices based on what you do or do not discover.

Know that you are not in charge of other people and cannot decide anything for them. You can only seek to understand them and offer enough of yourself so that they have an opportunity to understand you. Accept that others do not need to be perfect and neither do you. You are allowed to make mistakes and expand your understanding through participating directly and honestly while seeking to learn. It is important that you remain self-aware and accept your own experience and process. This approach eliminates the win/lose dynamic. It allows for differences to be what they are while you share, offer, gain understanding, test possibilities, and create boundaries. To acknowledge differences without judgment or competition is to respect individual experience and process. Recognize that diversity is the most natural occurrence or free flowing rule of life. When you accept the diversity of life you will experience greater trust and confidence.

From this section, is there anything that you can relate to in your own behavior? If so, write it down and explain some steps that you will take to transition yourself into a greater experience of self-awareness, self-acceptance, and acceptance of others. Also, what steps can to take to support the possibility of you understanding others while creating healthy boundaries.

_____
_____
_____
_____
_____
_____
_____
_____
_____
_____
_____
_____
_____

Transitioning Beyond Your Conditioned Blueprint

-31-

Understanding Anger and the Use of Rules

Anger can sometimes be useful. Beneficial anger supports a person in creating boundaries, and it can also be a protective force in the face of danger. Sometimes it propels a person into a process for change. The fierceness behind the anger can drive a person to challenge and overcome personal fears. However, unhealthy anger is more commonly expressed than beneficial anger.

Unhealthy anger often gets created and triggered by self-imposed rules that are inwardly experienced or projected out onto another person. These rules are based on wishes and desires that often have little to do with real options. There will always be personalization and judgment involved. A fantasy version of an experiential process and outcome are projected. Real options can only be realized through direct participation in the unfolding of actual experiences. Personalized rules cannot decide much about reality. They will not find a natural place in truth. They will likely only get fulfilled by force or by chance. This means that the rules would be accepted without question, or someone would submit to them from fear or conditioning.

In reality, what a person desires or wishes for may or may not be possible. When rules-based options are established on the basis of desire, they have no real foundation. Agreement upon fictitious stories is required for their continued existence. From this fictitious rule-based position, personalization, judgment, and blame will be used to decide what another person should be, should not be, or what they could have done. Judgments are used in an attempt to distort, predict, or decide an experience for other people. They block a person's ability to clearly perceive and understand someone else. One person cannot force their internal experience of anything onto another person's experience. When the other person complies, they are complying with an illusion. This usually takes place when an unconscious compulsive role becomes activated in response to the rule.

Once a person creates a judgment and projects blame, they put up a barrier that prevents them from connecting with themselves or another person or perceiving real options. They have replaced direct participation and discovery with fantasy. At this point, they become dependent upon a rule that came from their own or someone else's judgment. They have given up their own free will to the ideas within the rule.

As each moment of life unfolds, it is necessary to navigate many variables to weigh the best possible choices, gain understanding, and make new discoveries. A person can't do this if they are stuck in faulty beliefs and rules. Possibilities must be discovered from full participation in each individual experience and then weighed in relation to many factors within the larger picture.

Now, slowly contemplate this next part. There are two sides to this coin. On one side of this programming, a person identifies with a sense of false power through the use of personalized rules that are rooted in desire and judgment. They seek to force the use of these rules as a means of dominating and controlling others. Through entitlement and blame they personalize what others do or do not do in relation to the rules. Their entire exchange with other people is rule-based. The person forcing the rule is held captive by it as much as the person who feels forced to follow it. The one who created it is limited by the structure of their own desires, judgments, and the obedience with which others follow the rules. Relationships are expected to take place with the rules, not with the real people. There is no true connection or intimacy. The natural process of curiosity and discovery is halted; it is not even recognized. Because of a desperate need to predict all personal interactions, cooperation according to the rules is demanded. If a person does not oblige, it is perceived as an act of wrongdoing. The end result is compulsive anger and the creation of a drama. The aggressor takes on an unconscious self-appointed overlord position while passing out rules to those who are subservient or not. Association with a person through a basis of rules creates a paradigm where the individual is seen as good or bad instead of a person. Anticipation of the rules and participation with the rules becomes the primary relationship between the people involved. All other levels of relating are secondary. The actions of all involved parties will often be compulsive with little awareness of consequences to self or others. When something does go wrong, they will likely blame someone else. They may even manipulate another person into believing that they are responsible when in fact they are not.

On the other side of this, if a person is indoctrinated into believing in the personalized desire-based rules of others, they will automatically succumb to unacceptable circumstances. *They become conditioned to a fear of the possibility of false inescapable accusations of having done a wrong.* A belief in the possibility of being considered on an individual human level will have been surrendered to a state of personal powerlessness and subservience to the anger-driven rules. *The person will be paralyzed by their relationship with the rule.* In a situation of conflict, the option of deciding value and truth for the self will not be realized. The person may lose sight of their own values, beliefs, and needs in the moment through dissociation from the total experience. At the very least, their individual experience will be pushed into the background. Later, when they are out of the situation, they will become confused while wondering what happened. This can lead a person into self-judgment, self-doubt, and internalized anger toward themselves or the other person. They may develop internal fantasy scenarios of struggles to feel heard and seen. However, since they won't actually be heard or seen, a cyclical internal drama will play out to no end. The person may develop a relationship with the internalized fantasy-drama while feeling disdain and judgment toward the other person. This takes place because the person still feels powerless. No direct, honest sharing is taking place between real people to gain understanding, come to a resolution, and/or create boundaries.

Once an individual learns to relate to the closest people in their life in this way, the pattern often extends into their own relationship with the self. They may impose rules upon the self yet fear their own ability to follow the rules. This can happen through perfectionism. They may also develop obsessive thinking about good/bad options and behaviors such as being overly responsible for meeting the known or imagined needs of others, while overlooking their own needs. Or perhaps they have extreme beliefs about orderliness, exercise, or food. A person may believe that specific routines must be followed in a rigid manner. This can become obsessive-compulsive. In this case they will have transitioned the rule dynamic from its outside origins with the aggressor to their internal relationship with the self. This will create a barrier to direct inner personal experience and create some degree of internal drama.

Can you identify any externally expressed anger that came from desire and judgment-based rules within yourself or someone else? Can you identify any internalized anger that was created from fear and judgment-based rules in yourself? Now look at how the rules decide things for you in contrast to you choosing from the basis of true needs and values. Some examples of true needs and values may include what is purposeful, feelings, likes, dislikes, etc.

Can you identify how the rules limit your experience and possibilities?
_____
_____
_____
_____
_____
_____
_____
_____
_____
_____
_____
_____
_____
_____
_____
_____
_____
_____
_____

-32-

The struggle between victimhood and anger based, dominant behavior created from the use of rules and judgment

In this example a woman by the name of Lidia had a very structured upbringing with a father who was a Navy General and a mother who was an emergency room nurse. Her parents created rules and structure for everybody in the household and for most experiences. Therefore, individuality was a secondary consideration when approaching or planning most anything. The rules led the way. This simplified things for her parents.

Because of her history, Lidia learned to trust in the simplicity of structured planning and the relationship with the ideas within rules instead of considering the individual experience of each person. She prided herself on her ability to navigate problems and strategize a practical approach to many situations. She believed in the most ideally imagined possibilities for other people, but she did not really see other people for who they were. When she evaluated others through the construct of rules, she misinterpreted this as intimacy. When a situation did not proceed in the manner that she had imagined, she felt as though someone was doing something to her personally. She sometimes felt that other people were overlooking her needs or being deceitful, irresponsible, or inefficient. Her judgment and anger were activated which led to imaginary scenarios toward others. Most of this played out in her mind, making her feel like a victim. In her imaginary scenarios she was the angry self-righteous victim, and others were acting against her.

However, other people were only being themselves according to their own programming, strengths, and shortcomings. Even though the people in her life showed her who they were, as they interacted repeatedly in the same way, she still imagined that they should or could be different. However, they could not. The way that they were was all that they knew, and they were for the most part accepting of it. Her rigid analysis of others functioned as a weapon that worked against her ability to be free and spontaneous with others. She was tormented by this conditioned approach while imagining that others were wronging her. She functioned as the tormenter and the victim. She flip-flopped from angry to sad and sad to angry. Her historical lens had been adjusted to expect those around her to be the good people who followed the rules and obediently made the "right" choices. However, she was the sole creator of all the rules and could not perceive how unfitting it was to expect others to innately know and follow them without question. Her sense of self and safety were all wrapped up in this. She was attempting to pass on to others what her parents had passed on to her.

In a situation where there has been a lifelong pattern of judgment and anger, there will also be the unconscious experience of leading others to play an inferior, bad person, or victim role or being a victim oneself. This can play out within the psyche of one individual or between multiple people. These two levels will alternate in a struggle. For example, when others are dominated by judgment for not following the rules, they are likely to feel like a victim. When reasoning and an effort to gain understanding are missing, both parties may feel trapped in this dynamic.

The victim experience often goes further. When the person who created the rules gets personally caught up in their attachment to others not following the rules, they become the victim of their own anger. This will continue until they see past their faulty beliefs and their relationship with the ideas within the rules, instead of with other people. They must break free through curiosity to perceive new possibilities for authentic sharing.

The nature of unhealthy judgment and anger is to control or force – to seek instant gratification through the implementation of rigid ideas. This does not leave room for the possibility of discovery or individuality. When a person approaches life in this way, an untainted clean experience will not be recognized. They will not know what it is like to be part of an experience that naturally unfolds. They will often be impatiently attached to rigid timeframes. Because of this, their actions for change are often futile with attempts taking place in a black and white manner while a true unfolding process is not allowed.

When a person does enter into the steps of a process for discovery or change, their compulsive-judgmental anger will constantly interrupt their participation and discovery toward the new goal by presenting criticism or judgment when the outcome of any step is different than the projected desire. This patterned part of the self will become the inner bully and activate a victim role simultaneously in the same person. When the person's authentic experience is interrupted by their own inner critic, they may feel frustrated, defeated, or powerless. They may lose sight of the fact that the outcome of each step in any process is unknown until it has been lived. The outcome of any step can only be evaluated and navigated when it is revealed through the unfolding of a real time experience. When the victim level of the person gives in to the angry bully, the pattern is empowered, and more criticism is likely to come. At this point, the victim aspect of the person will be further attacked. It will struggle to regain its strength and then take another step or two before the angry bully steps in again. This dualistic internal struggle will endlessly repeat itself until the person sees the truth of it through vigilant curious observation and contemplation.

Anger and judgment keep a person trapped in the mind, attached to rules and ideas, so that they cannot access their naturally unfolding experience or a deep inner process. The mind's idea of a process is very different than what takes place naturally on an experiential level. The mind perceives an interpretation to be the whole experience – the beginning and the final result. If there is only an intellectual understanding of something, the mind on its own expects that idea to be the reality. It is very black and white. Whereas in the fullness of experience, through full participation, there will be a natural process for taking the idea further and applying it to life while taking many steps and making many discoveries. It is also necessary to contemplate the unfolding details alongside your beliefs and evaluate purpose or meaning with the overall experience. You must participate in a deep experiential process to access true knowing. This means that your understanding is taken beyond the conditioned mind. So how does someone transition beyond this judgmental, angry, rule-driven approach to realize their own authentic experience and gain the freedom to see others as they are?

Steps for transitioning beyond victimhood or a role of dominance created from the use of judgment and anger

1. First the person must recognize that they are suffering. Through that recognition they must take responsibility for discovering the source of the suffering by going within. Taking responsibility is a choice that must be consciously made.
2. Most often the person will need to engage their healthy warrior to maintain a commitment to participate in the discovery process. Remember that the active judgment/anger level of consciousness is resistant to discovery, change, and letting go of blame.
3. It will be necessary to apply curiosity to create space so that discoveries can be made.
4. When this type of programming has been long-term, the anger and judgment are compulsive. Initially, it will be difficult to catch the

compulsions in the highly charged moments or to create space needed and a sense of distance from them. Therefore, the best way to begin is by noticing the everyday judgments and criticisms that arise from your mind throughout the day. Because there is only a fleeting attachment to these types of judgments, space can more easily be created with them.

5. Set your intentions each day to notice these judgments and criticisms as they arise. Once you notice them, activate your curiosity to witness and discern the rules and beliefs contained within them.

6. Inner questioning can be useful. Present one question at a time. Let the question sit in the space of curiosity along with the reaction while you continue to witness both.

7. Example questions are as follows: What am I believing that is not true? What kind of rules have I created for someone else or for myself? Do I have the right to decide how another person should live or what their capabilities should be? Do I really want to govern my own experience as a dictator? Am I able to see how the rules are creating difficulties for myself and others? If I take away the judgment and rules, what do I see in the other person or in myself? Do I think that other people should be the same as me? Do I truly perceive individuality in myself or other people? Can I accept the uniqueness of each person along with their strengths and inadequacies while putting the rules aside?

8. As you proceed, it is important to stay curious and refrain from being overly attached, as an intense attachment will keep you in a superficial level of mind and does not support the curious state. If your observing practice becomes very difficult, then step away and go back to it later. It is fine to do this throughout the day in short intervals.

9. Accept the fact that insight or answers may or may not come while you are observing. What you need will eventually come, but it has no timeline. It may come quickly within hours, days, or weeks. It may also come at times when you are not observing. This occurs because once you activate the curiosity and wholeheartedly present a question, the door is left open.

-33-

When you let go of judgment and engage your curiosity, understanding will be your reward

Conflicts are likely to arise between individuals for reasons such as personalizing, judging, projecting one's own perspectives or history onto another person, etc. These are obstacles that get in the way of understanding. Understanding is essential. It provides a common ground between people even when ideas, preferences, or approaches are different. Lack of understanding can lead to confusion, conflict, dismissiveness, and an inability to feel safe or to purposefully engage. If an internal struggle ensues due to a lack of understanding, it is likely that one person will project their own meaning onto the actions or choices of another person. As well, they will expect the person to live by their own perceptions, values, and preferences. If this dynamic occurs, individual identities become merged while personal boundaries are lost. The one who is judging becomes dependent upon the other person to make the "right" choices according to their *own* projected judgments and rules. The judgments and rules are birthed from the act of personalizing another person's perspectives, actions, or ways of being.

When someone feels judgment coming from another person, they may try to avoid interacting with them. However, they are most often unaware of the rules that are being projected upon them by the other person. Those rules exist solely in the mind of the one who created them. The person who created them imagines that the other person does know or should know what the rules are and should abide by them. This can only create confusion, resistance, struggle, and division.

Sometimes a person's past experience will lead to a distorted perception of their present experience. For instance, if someone had a self-centered, unapproachable boss in the past who made their work life difficult, this can affect a person's later perceptions of anyone who seems similar. They may base their ideas of a new boss's whole identity on a single aspect of behavior that they associate with the past boss, making a blanket judgment. This can lead to faulty perceptions of the new boss as being all bad. If the boss is perceived in this way, then there will be no opening or space to discover what is real or not real. The one who is judging may become attached to a need to create drama and expose the boss's behaviors so that others will also reject him. The offender may secretly hope for the boss to be fired. Any of these desires will be fueled by their own distorted stories. This behavior will block the possibility of discovering the other person's true identity. If you take this approach, you will be funneling your perception of the other person through your own self-created stories. You will have no direct experience of them. You will be defining them through your own stories.

To resolve this, you must recognize the truth of what you are doing. Every person is a unique individual with their own history. They have their own way of processing, along with individual strengths and challenges. It is impossible for anyone to truly know another person. The bulk of every person's experience is inside of them; therefore, you cannot directly access a complete, authentic experience of anyone. Whatever they show you is a small part of their identity. However, you can seek to understand another person by engaging through curiosity. Full participation with curiosity requires that you let go of the judgment, as they cannot exist together. Therefore, put the judgment aside and activate your curiosity while accepting the reality that you must engage to discover some the uniqueness within each person.

When you have decided that you do not like someone, you can still connect with them as they are by putting aside the judgment. You lose nothing by doing this. Sometimes when a person disagrees with someone else, they feel that they must reject that person. This is unnecessary; you need only understand what is happening and let that be your starting point.

Once you put the judgment aside, engage your own curiosity. Take a moment to observe the person. Seek to establish an overview of them so that you can meet them as they are – not through your prior definition of them. When you put the judgment aside there is no longer a struggle.

To begin a conversation, you can start with an open-ended question that is appropriate to the situation. If the other person initiates the conversation, then repeat back to them something that they shared with you. This lets them know that you are present and willing to engage. You might say, "I see, or I hear you, or now I understand." From there, continue to maintain your curiosity. Seek to discover more than what you think you already know. Stay focused. Create appropriate boundaries within yourself by consciously choosing to stay present so that you do not slip into personalization or judgment. Consciously make note of the discovery process as it unfolds. What you think you know today may not be the reality tomorrow. There may be many similarities between people; however, the differences within each human being are vast and everchanging. There is always more to discover.

When relationships are approached in this manner, authentic connection is possible through ongoing curiosity, discovery, and understanding. Differences between personalities and beliefs may be great; however, people can still get along and respect one another. Through acceptance and respect of differences people can become unified in the diversity of individuality.

Chapter Ten

The Home Stretch

-34-

Acceptance vs. desire for something else

Acceptance simply means that you are acknowledging reality as it is. There is no approval or disapproval of it. You recognize it to be fact and let go of wishful thinking. You are not personalizing anything. You are not resentful or judgmental about the available or unavailable options, or the character of any person. You simply see things as they are. There is no struggle to force an experience or person to be something else. They are who they are. When you accept, you become open to understanding even when something is different or not rational. You let go of any tendency to blame. Blame carries a suggestion that someone else is responsible for you. Instead, you remain open to discoveries. In this way, you have the potential to understand yourself, your needs, and your choices more clearly than anyone else. Only you can be responsible for you. Through acceptance you will have clear vision. You will realize the true capabilities of a person and the possibilities of a situation. Your focus and perspectives will not be based in desire, which is fantasy. This is possible when curiosity replaces judgment. Curiosity opens you up to seeing the diversity among people and in all of life. Through clear discernment, the difference between fantasy and truth can be established. With this recognition comes greater tolerance and compassion. Acceptance of diversity makes apparent the unique history and process within each individual and situation. When differences among people are accepted, then respect and equality can exist.

As long as the diversity of human experience remains unconscious, a struggle for sameness will exist among people along with a sense of separation. Differences will likely be judged and seen as wrong, inferior, or superior some part of the time. These judgments turn into desire-based rules. When diversity is realized and embraced through acceptance and reverence, then wholeness is realized on a deep experiential level. This is beyond what most people identify with on a daily basis. Each expression of diversity is an expression of the Divine. The source is the same even though the expressions present differently.

-35-

Birthing yourself from a concept-based experience into the substance of life

When you are consciously present in the moment you are functioning with clear discernment of imagination and true facts. Your mind is not seducing you into a state of full immersion with projections of the past or future through judgments, desires, and stories. You are not separate from experiential presence. However, the majority of people do not function in this way on a continual basis; many are not even consciously aware of in-the-moment experience.

Because concept-based thinking is often limited by fixed ideas and void of authentic individual experience, fulfillment from it will be fleeting and unstable. People are led by their histories, learned behavior patterns, reactions, defense mechanisms, desires, etc. These are all containers of limited perception and will create resistance toward the present moment. When these associations habitually occur, the unconscious mind will automatically define and decide many things for the person. Therefore, a person's relationship with life becomes story-based and belief-based rather than being one of direct experience through direct participation, ongoing discovery, learning, and renewal. If people do not understand the nature of fixed ideas and reactions, they will function as traps rather than doorways for inner discovery and growth. As a result, judgment, blame, or helplessness will lead one's attention outside of the self with a sense of dependency on people and situations. When you function in the moment, you realize that all challenges and reactions create an opportunity for a person to become curious, to question, discover, and make new choices. Challenges which are initiated by reactions and discomforts are doorways for discovery, change, and renewal. With some degree of conscious participation, suffering will lead you to bring your focus inward to seek relief. Then realizations will come through the practice of curiosity, witnessing, and contemplation as outlined throughout this book. When this is routinely practiced, it will likely bring about a gradual waking up process into clear consciousness. Through this process you will have moments of breakthrough into deep knowing and wisdom. For most people, this is an ongoing evolution and rarely an instantaneous happening.

It is important to understand that this is an ongoing process. A commitment without resistance is best. The more you contemplate your relationship to attachment and suffering, the more you will realize the value of unattached presence. If you are unattached this does not mean that you don't care about people or life. It just means that you will be choosing from a basis of what is real rather than from a place of desire. You will accept reality as it is while implementing a willingness to continually discover, learn, and become more experientially aware. This process cannot be realized through the mind alone. It must be realized through conscious participation. You might be asking, "How did the attachment or ego state come about?" The following is a theory that is based on the initial experience of your soul consciousness entering a body at birth and feeling separate from source – Divine consciousness.

When an expression of the Divine, a soul, is birthed into a body, that particular expression of Divine consciousness identifies with the human body as a form. At that point, the wholeness or source from which it came becomes forgotten. Perception becomes funneled through a dependency-based type of micro-focus. This consists of perceptions of need or desire and objects or actions for fulfillment. The attachment can be physically, mentally, or emotionally based. An identification with the form gets reinforced as needs repeatedly arise. When needs go unmet for a span of time there is discomfort and a sense of amplified separation. This leads to patterns of desire, projection (imaginary ideas), resistance, and struggle. It is through this process that ego develops. Along with ego development comes a sense of personal "I" and a predominant relationship to outer circumstances, along with the need to predict, control, and over-identify in a possessive manner. These behaviors bring the focus outside of the self and encourage a wide range of emotions. The emotional effects are temporary as they appear and then disappear. Through this process a duality is birthed, and the conditioned consciousness of the personal-self forgets the Divine source from which all emerges – the source from which it was birthed.

A good analogy for this is with the waves of the ocean, which ebb and flow. A wave arises as an expression of the ocean and then merges back into its source – the ocean. Similarly, each person manifests as a unique expression of the Divine yet is still the source. When a person perceives a wave, they are identifying with the form – not the ocean. There is a conceptual illusion that the wave is separate or somewhat separate from the ocean, but it is not. It is perceived as a wave but exists as part of the ocean. It is a temporary expression through the appearance of form.

A likeness can be seen in the appearance and disappearance of each person's personal experiences as they arise and then fall away. They originate in the form of the person which came from and is always an expression of pure presence or source. The expression of an experience is just that from within the essence of pure presence. A person is never really separate from Divine consciousness or source. It is just perceived as that on a temporary basis when the expression of consciousness through the limitations of mind perceives itself as a form.

How does a person remember the true self – the oneness of Divine presence? When you function in presence, you have a glimpse of remembering. Most often the remembering requires an ongoing commitment to choosing presence over the stories of the mind. The effects are cumulative. Profound experiences sometimes occur which bring a deep knowing of the Divine. Profound realization will often lead to a natural transition into presence.

We are all aware of stories about people merging with the light or the essence of oneness. Descriptions of this are varied. This most often happens when a person's life is teetering, when there is overwhelming physical pain that goes on at length, or a person is pushed to the brink mentally, emotionally, and spiritually. Sometimes it happens through deep contemplation and spiritual practice. Sometimes it happens through a combination of these situation. One such example is as follows:

Susan V Kippen

This is an account of a young woman who suffered chronic painful attacks from undiagnosed gallbladder disease for seven years. Sometimes the attacks lasted for hours, and sometimes they would last for a whole day. She sought help from medical doctors to no avail. The doctors suggested that the pain was perhaps from trapped gas, a discomfort from ovulating, or maybe it was imagined. An accurate diagnosis was not given for many years.

It was impossible for this woman to do anything during those attacks except to lie in bed. The pain was unbearable. Through a desperate attempt to find relief from the pain, she refused to put her focus on it. Instead, she lay there saying the same prayer over and over and paying attention only to her breath. Through this practice, the pain became more and more distant from her until she had only a very vague awareness of it. Her predominant experience became one of peacefulness. This became her regular routine for transcending the pain. She would stay in that state sometimes for hours until the pain stopped. Without consciously realizing it, she had taught herself to completely surrender while going into a deep meditative trance-like state. This ability proved to be valuable for her throughout her life. This person is me, Susan.

The gallstone attacks continued to occur. On one occasion the pain lasted for two days. That experience of suffering proved to be the worst and the longest that I had ever experienced. My prayer was unyielding. As I prayed, my focus followed the rhythms of my breath with an awareness that at first shifted back and forth from pain to peace. The pain-relieving practice provided a place of solace. My practice utilized a clean focus and window into pure presence. On this particular occasion, the peacefulness grew to be all-encompassing as I felt myself move into an experience of nothingness while leaving all discomfort behind and transcending the physical pain and body completely. There was a beautiful calming peacefulness that came to be. A movement which seemed to pull what I knew to be myself away from the body merged me within a wholeness with all of creation. My known form ceased to exist. There was only the experience of brilliant Divine light – of being pure and blissful. The experience was of love beyond words. I was formless. Any sense of "I" as a separate entity in the universe was no more. There was only a wholeness and oneness as all – an awareness or knowing of what is. This is the place of the "I Am" consciousness of all – of universal truth where all possibilities exist before form. It is the source of human existence. It is the experience of pure being – a place of pure truth where illusion

Transitioning Beyond Your Conditioned Blueprint

does not exist. The experience was timeless. But then something else began to happen.

Suddenly there was a sense of a separation beginning to take place – a pulling away. A personal self was beginning to take form again. The sense of "I" as a person was taking shape and being pulled away from the brilliance – the blissfulness. There was an awareness of wholeness and separation. It was like being in two worlds at the same time. There was a feeling of strong resistance to leaving the pure state. It was blended with the blissfulness. Soon I was consciously aware of my body which felt light. I opened her eyes, once again present in the physical realm – with a gentle, glowing peacefulness. A deeper awareness of Divine presence, an active state of curiosity, and an ability to access wisdom stayed with me. However, over the weeks that followed, I realized that my personal conditioning from my upbringing was still there. This brought about a subtle sense of longing for the wholeness of Divine consciousness. Even though I did not totally understand what had happened to me, there was a longing to just be totally as one with/as Divine – without separation – without the confines of the human struggle. I became motivated to seek and find a consistent experience of pure consciousness. This took me through many years of inquiry into religious and metaphysical practices and spiritual belief systems. Inner inquiry was also an ongoing part of this. Gradually, I understood the complexities of my own conditioning. My ability to perceive the truth within myself and others became fine-tuned. Through an ongoing search and self-inquiry, I have realized that wholeness and Divine consciousness are always accessible in the present moment. Our true nature is pure presence.

This type of experience most often does not bring full spontaneous enlightenment to the person who experiences it but leaves them with a heightened awareness of the Divine presence in all of life. There is often a trust in the Divine – the source from which we all come. Even though most people will not experience the source of creation in this manner, you can still experience wholeness and peace as you learn to transcend the traps of your conditioning.

When you are fully present in the moment, you are in the experiential substance of Divine consciousness – the source of life. There is a natural discernment of truth and fantasy. Fantasy is not part of your foundation; it is an imaginary occurrence that you recognize and know to be such. As you discern the difference, you acknowledge it as an expression but do not become seduced by it. You see it occurring; however, it is recognized as a choice. You leave it out of your consciously chosen experience. Your experience does not come from the basis of an idea alone; you are the expression of a constantly unfolding experience that is infused with grace. That grace and spaciousness is the essence of Divine. The mind is not leading you through a process of selective identification and participation with isolated individual details at the expense of the whole. When you are present as the substance of being, there an innate openness to ongoing discovery, transparent authentic sharing, mutual understanding, acceptance of what is, natural boundaries, and respect for differences. This is also the experience of equality. There is no judgment, force, or ongoing struggle. These create separation and fantasy through projections. There is a clear discernment, but this is different than judgment. Discernment is not dependent upon a personal story, desire, or reaction. An inner trust gracefully guides one's choices and actions.

The majority of people do not recognize when they are present even though it is the most natural, fulfilling way to be. They just know that they feel good at times and often attribute it to something outside of themselves. When a person understands that the doorway is inside of them and it is not dependent on what is outside, then they are able to embrace the natural self more often. With practice, they can attain true intimacy with the self. This opens up the possibility of greater intimacy with others and all of life.

Can you imagine what it might be like to live the experience of equality through participating first with yourself and then with others in an honest, open, curious, receptive state that is not limited by labels, differences, gender norms, history, judgment of self and others, or cultural beliefs. You would have the freedom to live each experience openly without having it tarnished by preconceived ideas or expectations of sameness. The idea that people should be the same is an illusion that is maintained by the collective ego of mankind. It is not possible for anyone to be the same as anyone else. Conditioning determines perspectives, beliefs, and behavior patterns; it is varied in each human being. Preconceived ideas or judgments can prevent a person from truly perceiving the uniqueness of themself and another person. When you recognize each person as presence, then there is a natural harmony and understanding of the conditioned differences. There is no need to take on any part of another person's history as a personal challenge. You

Transitioning Beyond Your Conditioned Blueprint

clearly know when or if it is meaningful to participate or not. Sometimes it is not; however, there is no judgment when making this choice. You simply see the truth of what is presented; you create appropriate boundaries with acceptance of your own and the other person's unique path.

As an exercise, an open mic club is a great place to begin to challenge yourself to perceive and accept the individuality of each person. When performing at an open mic club, the people who choose to play their music and sing on stage are courageously offering individual talents and abilities that you will never see again from any other person at any other time in exactly the same way during your entire life. Can you contemplate how amazing this is? Other situations that offer opportunities to witness individual uniqueness are at a child's school play, on public transit, at the grocery store, or anywhere that people gather. If you practice observing in this way at first, then it will be easier for you to witness the diversity in each person as you participate directly with them in everyday life. If you judge or personalize others, then you will not clearly see their uniqueness. Experiment with this. See what discoveries you make.

Write them down here.

_____
_____
_____
_____
_____
_____
_____
_____
_____
_____
_____
_____
_____
_____
_____
_____
_____

-36-

A bridge well-built; writing your own conclusion

By now you will have likely realized that witnessing, curiosity, contemplation, discovery, participation, surrender, and acceptance are necessary for accessing the depth of experience within yourself and all of life. It is truly your bridge from concepts, reactions, desires, compulsions, resistance, etc. to the experience of truth, understanding, and the substance of being. It is through your own inquiry, curiosity, discoveries, and ongoing participation that you support your own authentic experiential unfolding with access to continued wisdom and enrichment. If you fully participated with the process provided in this book, you will likely have had many realizations and changes come about.

It is now time to reflect upon the changes that have taken place within you and understand how those changes came about. This will help you to anchor in the new process so that it will be easier to consciously access when you need it. Has your participation with this book transitioned the understanding and

Transitioning Beyond Your Conditioned Blueprint

experience that you have of yourself? It so, describe your realizations.

Susan V Kippen

Based on what you have learned from this book, how do you see yourself proceeding differently in your day-to-day life as well as with your goals and challenges?

Transitioning Beyond Your Conditioned Blueprint

Know that your journey does not end here. You write your own beginning and conclusion to every experience, each and every day. The process that you have learned and implemented is a recipe for life. At some point it will become natural. Remember that growth and transformation do not happen in a straight line. When difficulties come just keep going. As your journey toward greater presence continues, realizations will be an ongoing part of your life.

Biography

Susan Kippen has been a practicing Holistic Healer and self-awareness teacher for more than three decades. Her empathic and intuitive abilities emerged early in life. As a young adult, an interest in self-awareness, alternative health, and spirituality led her to realize that she could utilize her natural gifts to help others. Through a profound spiritual experience, a deep connection to the Divine in all things was realized. Susan's ability to perceive the depth of experience within others allows her to guide them with wisdom. Over the years she has developed a unique holistic therapeutic approach that has proven to be effective with thousands of clients.

Through her holistic healing practice, South Shore Natural Healing, she teaches self-awareness, provides guidance for the reprogramming of faulty beliefs, offers Polarity Therapy, Hypnosis, Reiki, Shamanic techniques, remote healing, and space-clearing. During sessions with clients, Susan works from a pure state of presence to merge with the foundational truths behind their active emotional states to help them to understand the complexities of their conditioning while giving spiritual guidance for personal growth and transformation. Susan gained much of the knowledge and understanding offered in this book through her own spiritual seeking and personal growth as well as through the deep spiritual work and guidance that she has provided for others.

She works with clients all over in the world. She has offered educational classes of many types that include: teachings for self-awareness; all levels of Reiki; manifestation techniques; spirit clearing; meditation; and basic polarity techniques. She is a Certified Polarity Therapist, Reiki Master/Teacher, Hypnotist, TAT practitioner, and Holistic Healer. Susan also has a BA from UMass Boston;

however, her foremost credentials come from the experience of presence and the use of her natural abilities within the experience of life. Her professional goal is to assist individuals in seeing the truth within themselves and to be unafraid of their internal experience, so that they can grow and flourish in the celebration of life.

Made in United States
North Haven, CT
06 February 2023